Electronic Treasury Management

a guide for corporate and bank treasurers

Peter Gallant

Woodhead-Faulkner · Cambridge

Published by Woodhead-Faulkner Ltd
Fitzwilliam House, 32 Trumpington Street, Cambridge CB2 1QY, England
and 51 Washington Street, Dover, NH 03820, USA

First published 1985
© Peter Gallant 1985
ISBN 0 85941 273 3

Library of Congress Cataloging in Publication Data
Gallant, Peter
    Electronic treasury management.
    Includes index.
    1. Corporations – Finance – Data processing. 2. Banks
and banking – Data processing. 3. Money market.
I. Title.
HG4026. G35 1984   658.1′5′02854   84-15376
ISBN 0-85941-273-3

Designed by Ron Jones

Typeset by Hands Fotoset, Leicester

Printed in Great Britain by St Edmundsbury Press, Bury St Edmunds, Suffolk

Contents

Acknowledgements

I would like to thank the various members of the management of Citibank for their permission to reproduce examples of the computer output that appear in several of the descriptions of the electronic banking services that form a large part of this book.

I would also like to thank Graham Simister and Michael Smith for allowing me to use their computer program that is given in the Appendix.

Introduction

This book is written for two reasons. Firstly, to look at how information technology is changing office life, and secondly, to describe how financial markets work. Therefore this book hopes to explain to financial managers the use of electronic technology in solving everyday problems and to outline to technologists how the financial markets work, so that they can better appreciate how these problems are caused.

The book is written with the treasurer primarily in mind, either the treasurer of a bank or the treasurer of a corporation. The treasurer is at the 'sharp end' of the company, the interface between the company and one of the most important parts of its environment, the financial markets. Treasurers have two sets of problems, the collection and management of information and the execution of transactions caused by or anticipating that information. This information is often derived from transactional data fed into the company's mainframe computer systems. The availability of the information may be subject to considerable time delays as the data are often processed to meet other priorities first.

The information demanded by the financial managers concerns external events – for example, movements in foreign exchange rates – and internal requirements, such as a profile of the company's debtors or creditors. The usual computer-based financial systems tend to concentrate on the accounting and auditor requirements of the company, keeping the books and controlling the paper flows. These are essential to any business enterprise, but represent static and historical information. Ageing of receivables is a good example. It is an important piece of financial information and the proper collection of receivables is an important activity, with well established and widely understood techniques. Most managers are comfortable with the use of technology in this kind of application and the extensive use of computers to perform these functions is now almost taken for granted.

Managers are used to receiving and contemplating historical data. Financial business has, however, become far more dynamic in recent years and timing is of the essence in rapidly changing, volatile markets. Money changes in value every second of the day and needs to be carefully managed. New skills are being developed to meet these problems and these skills are represented in the treasury function, which may be performed by a separate, defined group of people or may be part of the general financial management of the company if the amount of activity does not justify a separate department.

The treasurer is responsible for the management of the company's money, which includes the raising of loans and the investment of surplus funds. Movements of cash, often over national boundaries or through other currencies, have to be managed and liquidity assured to enable transactions to be effected in a timely fashion. Liquidity management requires forecasts of both cash flow and likely movement in market rates. The more liquid the balance sheet, the greater will be the requirement for tight treasury control.

Modern small business systems and electronic banking extend the possibilities for companies of any size to make better use of the financial markets to reduce the cost of using money in the business. Financial managers should keep abreast of developments in technology, as each advance in communications improves the basic essentials of cash management and treasury activities.

A company large enough to have a treasury function will have a computer managing its book-keeping and information systems. Modern folklore defines a computer as an imposing collection of gleaming, hostile machinery housed in glass-walled, controlled environments and attended by large numbers of serious, white-coated, alarmingly young operators. The machines talk in special languages, take a long time to gather momentum and are subject to bizarre breakdowns. The way the machines are used tends to be imposed on the company by the data processing managers, the only people who can talk to the machines, rather than in response to the needs of the users. Once introduced, computer-based procedures are difficult to change, and changes take a long time, usually so long after the original request for information that an adequate, but time-consuming, alternative has to be found to provide the solution in the meantime.

These problems between users and technologists are commonplace. Both sides are usually at fault, as neither the data processing manager nor the financial manager understands or takes time to understand the other's problems or business environment. The relationship is changing. Modern computers allow the financial manager access to considerable processing power without having to use the mainframe. Treasurers will use small business systems increasingly, as they are flexible and easily programmed. The treasury function should no longer be dependent on external development of computer systems and the present-day treasurer should be aware of off-the-shelf software packages and the electronic banking services offered by banks. However, it would be far more sensible to use these facilities to supplement the mainframe capability. The question as to who should control the development of small business systems, which paradoxically have the greatest application in large corporations, is occupying a central place in the discussion of how companies should be organised in the future. If it is to be the data processing manager, he will have to understand the needs of his constituents more completely, introduce flexibility and quick response times and dedicate resources accordingly.

Small companies do not have these problems with demarcation, but neither will they have resident experts to evaluate and install the equipment needed for modern financial management. The pace of change is bewildering, but must be understood if the company is to get value for money and any advice must be treated with a healthy scepticism, particularly if it is being offered by a hardware salesman.

A business is represented by its products, its services and its people. The numerical description of the company and its activities is expressed in financial terms. Financial activities are mathematical by nature and so perfectly suited for computer analysis. As computers become more flexible and user friendly they are coming out of the back office and on to the desks of the salespeople, the traders and dealers, and the managers of the company. As money becomes more and more complex to manage, computer processing of financial data will inevitably grow.

Many people are uncomfortable using computers. However, interaction with them is almost unavoidable. We come across them directly when we use machines such as cash dispensers or indirectly when we use articles produced as a result of computers, such as robot-painted motor cars. Computers are controlled by microprocessors, which have become both cheap and powerful. Microprocessors are also being used more and more to control our household and personal equipment, from car engines to digital watches, washing machines to microwave ovens.

The development of microprocessors has led to the introduction and incredible growth in unit sales of personal computers, making data processing accessible on a consumer rather than a professional basis for the first time. All managers should be conversant with personal computers and the impact they could have on the working environment. For business purposes, a personal computer should be defined as a fairly serious machine, such as an Apple IIe or an IBM-PC with disc-based memory; Spectrums and Vic-20s are fine for the family, but too slow and frustrating for a business user.

There is no acceptable substitute for 'hands on' experience, which demonstrates both the strengths and the shortcomings of the machine in question. Many of the problems of financial management can now be solved using personal computers and understanding computers is both enjoyable and productive. Computer literacy is growing steadily more important every day, but cannot be learned properly from a printed page. If this book does nothing more than arouse sufficient interest in managers to get more closely involved with using technology in developing their own solutions, then it will have served its purpose well.

The first part of this book looks at the technology that now surrounds the treasurer, at how computers and telecommunications work, and at the changes taking place in the industries that provide the equipment. In the second part we look at the financial markets, in particular the money markets and foreign exchange markets, and how a bank treasurer uses technology to manage his dealing activities. In the third part we look at the corporate treasurer and how electronics are now playing an increasingly important part of his day-to-day business activities.

Part One

The treasurer
and computer technology

CHAPTER 1

The role of the treasurer

Money plays a central role in the lives of most people. Making money is the main reason that motivates people to work. The success of the companies that employ those people is measured in terms of money. Money has to be considered not just as a means of motivation and measurement but also as a basic raw material that changes in value constantly: it has to be managed in the same way that any valuable asset has to be looked after and maintained. The management of money is no simple problem and requires many different skills to be done properly. Companies employ accountants to track down the way that money is used and earned; financial managers ensure that companies have enough money to keep the business going; treasurers are employed to manage the money itself.

In this book we are interested in the treasury function and the way that that activity should be managed. Managing money through a treasurer and his department is a relatively recent development for most UK companies, but the need to manage money in an intelligent way is now recognised as a separate skill from those of the more traditional financial management areas. This increase in prominence of the treasurer in the general management of the company is taking place during a time of radical change in office administration caused by developments in technology and the changing natures of the computer and telecommunications industries. We will look at the concerns of commercial companies and banks, the major users of money when it comes to the management of their treasuries, within the context of these changes. We will therefore be looking at two distinct types of treasurer, the bank treasurer and the corporate treasurer, who have quite different business needs.

Treasury functions

The treasury function divides into two main activities. Firstly, there is the collection of information concerning the movement of money throughout the company, including future inflows and outflows, and the execution of transactions called for in response to that information. Secondly, there are control and management responsibilities, both towards the treasury's own activities and also the general business of the company. While the bank treasurer is chiefly concerned with controlling the risk associated with a large number of financial transactions, the corporate treasurer's function can be simply defined as cash management in all its aspects, from raising financing to controlling foreign exchange exposure in the most effective manner. As a discipline the treasury department draws together and redefines many functions traditionally carried out in staff and line departments around the company, mostly in the management and financial accounting areas.

The more liquid the balance sheet of the company, the more critical is the role of the treasurer. Thus the treasuries in banks and trading companies are key profit centres, while the treasuries in manufacturing companies are usually considered staff functions. While many consistently successful companies, particularly the major multinationals, have well established, large treasury departments, some companies still consider treasury to be a 'new' management task and generally understaff the activity in terms of numbers and quality of people. It is likely that staff functions will be kept lean and in common with other staff areas, the treasurer will have to rely on electronics and automation to keep pace with an increasingly complex environment.

Although most of the central staff functions will decline over time, the importance of the treasury function is almost certain to increase, even if many of the day-to-day activities will be controlled and executed in the subsidiaries rather than by a central treasury department. The continuing changes in the structures of both the domestic and international financial markets will require co-ordination of banking facilities and investment of surplus funds. The treasurer can therefore expect to take on more and more work with little opportunity to increase the number of people working for him; he will have to rely on computerised systems to manage the work load.

In general terms the trend in the UK is a continuing one towards centralisation of treasury functions. Treasury departments are usually seen as cost saving rather than profit generating, which leads to conservatism and stifled imaginations. This is a pity, as intelligent management of reasonable and quite small risks can produce spectacular, if sporadic, results and adds greatly to job satisfaction. The treasury function tends to be viewed as operational rather than executive and policies are often ill-defined.

Investment

Through its cash budgeting process a corporation will determine the likely surpluses and deficits for the budget period. The corporation then must decide how to use the forecast surpluses, and at the same time, ensure it is able to cope with miscalculations in timing or unexpected cash requirements. As well as setting policies for the investment process, the company should have clearly defined procedures as to how to invest its surplus cash.

Investment income, while possibly a valuable contributor to earnings, is usually outside the mainstream of corporate activity, as normal business should yield a higher return than that available from investments of cash. Short-term investment must be properly controlled and criteria established to cover risk, liquidity and return.

Risk must be considered for three possibilities: credit risk, country risk and foreign exchange risk. The credit risk for banks and financial institutions is difficult for an outsider to understand as these businesses have large revenue streams, very thin margins, relatively small fixed assets and low net worth when compared with industrial companies. A major investor should establish credit lines for the financial institutions and their instruments: allocation of lines by investors must consider the overall exposure worldwide of the company to each borrower. If depositing with a domestic financial institution, such as a finance house, which would tend to pay higher rates than a major bank, the depositor should be keenly aware of the type of business that the company is involved in and should pay particular attention to the way that the finance house manages its financial affairs.

Liquidity means having enough cash to meet known requirements, un-expected requirements and emergencies. In general terms the investor should look for the greatest return possible, consistent with the criteria established for risk and liquidity, and take into account the overall taxation structure of the company.

The investing company usually draws up a set of investment rules, including a list of those people delegated to invest (or borrow) funds on behalf of the company, with their individual powers and limits. This will protect each party involved, including the company, by clearly specifying each individual's part in the investment or borrowing process.

The company will look to reduce to a minimum any risk involved in the placing of an investment. This can be done by only investing in an agreed list of names, facilities and instruments; by diversifying holdings to minimise the impact of any credit failure; by always covering any foreign exchange exposure, unless all parties involved in the investment decisions are agreeable to leaving the investment uncovered; by diversifying overseas holdings to reduce country risk to a minimum; and by ensuring that all tax and legal implications, particularly with cross border investments, have been considered.

Cash management

Cash management traditionally has been concerned with cash balances and the two mainstreams affecting cash flow, receivables and payables. Receivable collection remains firmly a function of the management accountants, and is usually decentralised as much as possible. Management of payables is usually part of the purchasing department, whose main concern is not to upset suppliers. Treasurers have a reasonably clear idea of when money is going out or can collect that information easily enough, but have little control over the timing of incoming funds. For this reason most companies tend to have a positive cash balance to manage their working capital and the greater part of this is on current account or overnight deposit. Longer-term investments are avoided because of this uncertainty, but more importantly because of the lack of recognition the additional income would receive from senior management, who may be more concerned with the liquidity risk implied by the investment.

Centralisation of cash management becomes more important with the degree of international business that the company is involved in. A company trading only in the UK can co-ordinate its cash business through using a single clearing bank and netting out intergroup credit and debit balances to come to a consolidated figure for the overall company. This is not the type of service that most clearing banks would offer as a matter of course, especially if the sub-sidiaries deal with a geographically wide spread of the bank's branches. Apart from intercompany netting, there is a marked shortage of cash management services offered by the clearers to their UK-based clients.

Foreign exchange and cash management increase in sophistication as companies grow in size and the need for specialised dealers is recognised. Foreign exchange policies are normally set within the context of prevailing market conditions, and an important part of the treasurer's function is the preparation of forecasts based on his discussion with banks and economists. Most companies have realised the necessity for selective forward cover, but some still cover everything, following a policy that considers the opportunity loss that such an action leads to is better than having to manage the risk of an open position.

The use of Reuters monitors is slowly increasing, but most companies find that the cost is not offset by any increased efficiencies: swift collection of market information is of little use to a non-risk-taker. Most companies cover foreign exchange requirements as they happen and the auditor's influence can be seen in standard procedures that say that several banks have to be called at the same time to get the best rate, although delaying placing the deal for a few hours could create much more substantial benefits.

Risk management

Paradoxically, the treasury function is not perceived as a risk management activity in a corporation, whereas in a bank it could easily be the central point for risk management. The company treasurer is bound by senior management to be conservative and has little scope to try new ways to reduce the exposures that the company may have. However, by taking intelligent positions or by aggressively managing the cash movements under his control the treasurer can substantially improve the wealth of his company.

One problem may have been that with the comparatively small numbers of people working in the treasury department, the treasury function is often neglected in terms of dedicated office systems. With the computer-based products now available from many banks this problem should no longer apply.

The treasurer in action

To get a feel for the world of the treasurer let us look at some of the day-to-day activities of the people who work in the treasuries of banks and corporations. To see how these groups of people interact we shall follow the course of a fairly complex financial transaction between the treasurer of a company looking for trade finance and the dealers of a commercial bank. As we move through the transaction we will cover most of the elements which will be discussed in greater detail in later parts of this book. The size and type of the two main protagonists involved, the trading company and the bank, are not particularly relevant to the discussion, but we will assume that both are large and have a substantial presence in the international markets.

The corporate treasurer will have reporting to him one or more dealers responsible for executing the purchase and sale of foreign exchange contracts with the banking system, the investment of cash, (probably in several currencies) and the day-to-day administration of borrowing facilities. A separate part of the treasury will be responsible for arranging those borrowing facilities and for recommending the amount that can be invested in any particular company or instrument. A third function will cover the management of cash, including the setting of policies for hedging exposures created by the ever-changing rates in the markets. The bank treasurer will have dealers working in all the markets in which the bank operates, totalling from around five or six people in a small bank to between 50 and 100 in a major bank. While some dealers will be very specialised, for example, trading in gilt-edged securities, others will be generalists, providing a wide range of services for the corpcrate customers of the bank. The bank treasurer will be closely concerned with the book-keeping system to ensure that his business is being correctly reported, particularly where changes to instruments or the introduction of new instruments is concerned. As the book-keeping entries mostly originate from the dealers the proper and timely management of transaction processing is a critical task, requiring as least as many support personnel as there are dealers.

Setting the scene

Before we look at the transaction itself let us set the scene by looking at the offices of the treasurer of the company and the dealing rooms of the bank. Assuming it is around 7 a.m. on a typical working day it is unlikely that the individuals in either institution will yet be at their desks, although the dealing rooms will start to fill up shortly after 8. If the markets had been really wild it is quite possible that dealers would have been in earlier to settle their positions in the Far East markets.

As the corporate treasurer is so involved with international trade and the consequent requirements of both the parent company and its overseas subsidiaries, he has in his office the modern tools of his trade, a Reuters monitor and its attendant keyboard. In the outer office a clerical assistant has a terminal that can be connected to the data base of the company's main bank. Another clerk has a terminal plumbed into the company's own computer system. The secretary is equally equipped with electronic assistance. A telex and a facsimile transmitter supplement the more usual forms of letter and telephone communication. The secretary's word processor would be a powerful computer by any standard, and its output comes off a high quality printer. Copies are taken on a fast photocopier machine that can enlarge or reduce the copies taken of the documents; copies are fed into a collator that sorts the documents into sets as required.

Impressive as all this hardware may be, the modern treasury office has some way to go to catch up with the electronic equipment needed to operate even a small dealing room. With the exception of some small bourses in Europe, trading in money and foreign exchange has grown with the spread of telephones and telexes; very few transactions are concluded face to face, in marked contrast to the older commodities and stock exchanges. The dealer's desk is therefore a mass of communications equipment. Noiseless telephones indicate calls by means of flashing lights on the boards in front of the dealers. Many of these lights are connected to lines that link directly to brokers, banks and customers, who are called simply by pressing the button that masks the flashing light. In addition to the Post Office lines the dealer has several internal lines, used to talk with customers who are connected through the bank's switchboard or with other parts of the bank, particularly the operational back-up for the dealing team. In a large room the dealer will have in addition a private intercom system linking him to the other dealers in the dealing room or to dealers and support staff in other parts of the building.

Most dealers sit in front of multiple video screens, showing market information or pages of data generated by the bank's computers. The dealer may take both the Reuters and the Telerate information services. Specialists will take information from other sources, which provide, for example, charts of rate movements, delivered, like Reuters and Telerate, electronically. He also gets rates from brokers, all of whom are probably allocated direct telephone lines. Brokers operate between banks, putting buyers and sellers together for a small fee based on the size of the transaction. As they are constantly in the market they provide a continual stream of up-to-date information. Some will be listened to at all times through brokers' boxes, loudspeakers connecting the broker with the bank, which broadcast the broker's general conversations to the dealing room; if the dealer likes what he hears he can interrupt a conversation to see if he can get a piece of the action for himself.

Many markets, especially the foreign exchange markets, deal virtually 24 hours a day, so the dealers in the banks tend to start earlier than their customers. At around 8 a.m. the dealers start to straggle in. If he were losing money or hopeful of a profit then a dealer would probably be in earlier. The dealers come in and try to assimilate their position by checking the news and rate information collected while they were asleep. They settle down to a low hubbub of noise, using the strange jargon of the money and foreign exchange markets. The room is split functionally, with money market, foreign exchange and customer dealers grouped together. A large room will have between 40 and 80 dealers, creating several thousand transactions a week. As the morning goes on the noise levels rise as the telex operators and the support staff begin to arrive.

At about this time the treasurer and his staff have arrived in the office and are looking at the problems that the day will bring. They know already that they will have to raise trade finance to cover a shipment of goods overseas. The treasurer is well aware that he can get bargains from time to time if he looks carefully at the market. He can find these bargains by watching the same information services used by the bank's dealers and by developing good business relationships with his contacts in the bank's dealing room.

By the time the treasurer and his assistant are ready to go into the market and raise the finance needed for a particular trade transaction the London money and foreign exchange markets are in full swing. To illustrate how he can use the markets let us assume that the treasurer's problem concerns the financing of a shipment of goods that have been sold in US dollars, with payment due in 60 days' time. As the company is based in the UK it needs to borrow sterling to cover the period until payment is received.

Doing the deal

Let us think about the implications for communications that this transaction raises. Firstly, the treasurer needs to get a handle on the rates that now apply in the market. He may get this by looking at the Reuters monitor, by calling up several banks or by a combination of both. If the treasurer has contacted the bank the dealer will have to get rates from four quite separate markets, although each is dependent on the others. These are the London and New York money markets, the spot foreign exchange and the forward foreign exchange markets. Some of these rates he can get from other dealers in the bank by calling out or by using an intercom. When he has to go out into the market he will make contact over the telephone, by pushing a button on a direct line to connect him to a broker or his New York branch. He may contact New York over the telex – dollar/sterling foreign exchange is known as 'cable' to the dealers, as this was the source for most price quotations when telephones were more difficult to use. He will use an intercom or internal telephone call to check the credit line for the customer and possibly the spread or mark-up that he should add to the financing cost to compensate the bank for the risk it undertakes by providing the finance.

The dealer will contact the treasurer with a range of financing and foreign exchange options. If the treasurer accepts one of the offers then the dealer puts in train a second wave of activity. Cables will have to be sent to confirm moneys raised in New York. These go into a message switch that formats telexes and test words automatically and acts as a relay station, sending and receiving messages to or from every country in the world. The operations group, which for most banks in London is several miles away from the centre, must be informed quickly, probably by sending a facsimile copy of the instructions down the telephone, so that the transactions can be processed.

Telexes may have to be sent to other banks advising movements of funds. The customer's accounts have to be debited or credited. An advice note will be sent to the customer and will probably cross in the post with a confirmation letter sent by the treasurer to the bank. Both the bank and the company will have to pass the entries necessary to record the transactions, including the adjustment by the bank of the company's credit lines. The several dealers involved will have to adjust their various positions and this could cause a flurry of activity in the market if the transaction is large. These in turn create more book-keeping entries. Rates may change and these will be reflected on the treasurer's Reuters screen.

Let us return to the treasurer of the trading company and see how he goes about solving his problem. He needs to borrow sterling to finance a shipment of goods; in 60 days' time he will receive US dollars in settlement of the shipment. He is dealing on open account. If he were dealing with a company that he did not know or which was not considered creditworthy then the trading company may have insisted on a letter of credit, whereby a bank would stand between the customer and the supplier. Financing could then be arranged by discounting the drafts delivered as part of the documentation of the letter of credit.

Companies can borrow money in a multitude of ways. Long-term money can be raised on The Stock Exchange through equity issues or the sale of debentures, although debentures are unfashionable at the present time. Medium-term debt, up to ten years, can be borrowed from banks or raised through the Eurobond market, with the bonds underwritten by the banking system and sold to private or corporate investors. Term debt is normally restricted with covenants and carries a premium to reflect the credit risk being undertaken by the lenders. Short-term financing for working capital can be raised through overdrafts or the discounting of trade paper, whereby the financial markets finance the particular transaction.

The treasurer is looking for working capital. He can borrow either dollars or sterling. He can borrow either on overdraft, where the interest rate will fluctuate with the bank's base rate, or on a two-month loan, with the rate fixed for the period. If he thinks interest rates will fall then he will be tempted to use the overdraft. Alternatively he could raise either US dollar or sterling bankers' acceptances, which are promissory notes that have the name of a first-class bank added to assure the market of the credit risk. The acceptances can be sold in the market, usually at a discount, so that the interest is taken out of the amount being lent. The acceptance market is large and liquid, and because the creditworthiness of the instruments is of a high order, it is often a very cheap place to raise finance.

If the treasurer decides to use US dollar bankers' acceptances then he will need to have an arrangement with the London bank to issue paper in New York without having to wait for the drafts to be delivered through the mail for acceptance by the bank in New York, as the rate will be fixed only on the day the drafts are received, assuming the bank still has time to deliver the paper to the buyers in the market. He has the same problem with sterling bankers' acceptances if he is situated outside the London area.

We are contemplating the use of one of several instruments available in two currencies. We will see later that by using foreign exchange we can, at no risk, substitute a dollar borrowing for our sterling needs. This riskless activity, which is the cheapest way to use one market in substitution for another, is called arbitrage. It is the natural, economically rational action taken by traders at any time that the rates in one market move out of line with the rates in another; arbitrage is the means by which the relationships between disparate instruments are maintained. As we look at the money markets remember that there is usually a quantitative relationship that can be determined between one instrument and another. We will need to find a method to work out quickly the way to compare one instrument with another if we are to indulge in arbitrage, which can be a very rewarding activity.

The treasurer of the trading company has the choice of borrowing any currency to finance his need for working capital. For the purposes of simplicity we will assume that he will limit his review to sterling and US dollars, although if he were more adventurous he may wish to look at borrowing instruments denominated in other currencies. He can borrow his dollars in London through the Eurodollar market or, as this is a trade transaction, on the domestic money market in New York through a bankers' acceptance. He may be able to raise even cheaper domestic dollars, but this would be unusual, as even the largest UK companies have baulked at tapping the cheapest form of domestic US dollar financing, commercial paper, due to the cost and 'hassle' associated with getting a credit rating from the two main rating agencies, Moody's and Standard and Poor.

Apart from evaluating the cost of the different instruments he must also decide if he wishes to accept an exposure in foreign exchange. He has one at the beginning, as he will be paid in dollars in 60 days' time. If he borrows sterling to meet his immediate needs and the value of the dollar falls against sterling then he will not get sufficient cash inflow to repay his sterling obligation.

The treasurer can get around this sort of problem by using the standard techniques available to him on the foreign exchange markets. Forward foreign exchange exists to hedge future cash flows. Forward swaps permit arbitrage between one currency and another, with all the costs predetermined through the swap, thus he can borrow sterling through a dollar bankers' acceptance without exposing himself needlessly to foreign exchange risk.

When the treasurer is ready to place his business he calls the bank and speaks to the marketing officer who looks after his account. In this instance he will probably speak directly to the dealer who looks after his foreign exchange and short-term money market transactions. The customer dealer sits in the same room as the interbank dealers who are making markets in the currencies with other banks. After some discussion on how best to structure the financing the dealer collects the information needed to evaluate the different ways that the finance could be arranged. He calls through to the funding dealers for sterling and dollar LIBOs (the wholesale costs of funds) for the 60-days period; the dollar LIBO is the Eurodollar rate. The sterling dealer will also give him the sterling bankers' acceptance rate for the same period. A call to New York will get a dollar bankers' acceptance rate; if New York is not yet open it will have posted an overnight rate, but this will be weighted to reflect expectation of possible interest rate movements. As interest rates are less volatile these are collected first.

Now the customer dealer calls for foreign exchange rates. First he goes to the forward dealer who gives him the points needed to come to the 60 days forward rate. He then gets his spot cable, the dollar/sterling exchange rate. The rate is only good for a short period and the customer dealer has to keep the spot dealer advised if the rates are still out under offer to enable the rate to be changed if necessary. The interbank dealers are all exposed at this time and the customer dealer must fill his order quickly and report to the four dealers involved in the shortest possible time. If the treasurer chooses to deal then all four dealers have new transactions that could affect their positions. The most critical could be that of the spot cable dealer, which suffers the widest swings in rate movements, and therefore in profits, among the dealers involved.

Let us assume that the treasurer of the trading company and the customer dealer have agreed to use the cheaper of dollar or sterling bankers' acceptances to fund the company's need for sterling working capital. The dealer has got the rates needed to compare the cost of the instruments. To calculate the comparative costs he must bear in mind the following points.

1. Bankers' acceptances are quoted at a discounted rate and these rates will have to be converted to a true yield to compare them to the LIBO rates.
2. Yields must therefore bear in mind the lost opportunity of paying interest at the front end, on the day that the bankers' acceptances are arranged.
3. Sterling is quoted on a 365-day basis and dollars on a 360-day basis.
4. Spreads, that is, the bank's margin, will be different for the different instruments.

The dealer could perform the necessary mathematics keeping in mind all of these things with a calculator. He is probably better served using a micro-computer, which will not only quickly compute the rates, but will also store the rates for future reference and can easily be programmed to produce the deal tickets recording the transaction.

The placing of the series of transactions that will make up the financing for the trading company will set in train a number of funds movements through the banking system. These will join the thousands of funds transfers that take place every day in the local financial markets. Some of these will be for very small amounts, some will be so substantial that they may require special handling.

Moving money needs to be managed carefully. Before there were the facilities to move money by cable, any funds transfer had to be made in physical gold or cash; this was both tiring and dangerous. Cheques may be more secure, but are less immediate. To speed up the value date for cleared funds for a large cheque it may be cheaper to send it by air courier to its country of origin rather than wait for the normal air mail to take its course. Air couriers and messengers carry pieces of paper between one bank and another, speeding up the time needed for the settlement of payments.

But as gold and cash gave way to pieces of paper, so paper is now increasingly being replaced by electronic funds transfers. Couriers and messengers are needed less and less as the paper-less banking system takes over. Understanding how the money moves about is the first step towards intelligent cash management. This process is undergoing some major changes as automation becomes used more and more and procedures are standardised throughout the banking system. Each time money is moved or exchanged there is a cost involved. Cash management is concerned with reducing that cost by speeding up the time taken to transmit funds, by seeking the cheapest possible way to transfer the funds or by reducing cash flows to remove the need for unnecessary foreign exchange.

All of these factors affect the treasurer in his day to day activities: he should welcome the assistance that new technology will bring.

CHAPTER 2

Development of computers

The pace of change in office technology is so swift that only the youngest of managers will have had computer science included in his general education. The growth of computer-based services has been so rapid that very few computer specialists have crossed over into other areas of management and those who have are usually entrepreneurs who set up their own businesses. Computers are therefore viewed by non-specialists either as part of a service provided by a remote group of technicians or as complex pieces of equipment understood only by enthusiasts.

All companies of any size use computers, yet even today very few managers have any idea as to how those computers work or are able to participate intelligently in any discussion concerning computers. As as ill-informed user the manager will be asked to agree to systems that could radically affect the work-flow of the people under his supervision, but will not be able to forward his own views as to the best means to implement these plans. Equally important is the proper understanding of communications systems with all the potential changes, both commercial and social, that could follow the introduction of wider and faster telephone and data transmission networks.

Basic principles of computers

Computers are really quite simple things, made mysterious only because it is not possible to see what is going on, as all the activity takes place in electronic circuits. The development of computers has been constrained by physical rather than intellectual considerations and the rapid changes we are now used to seeing were only possible once certain physical limitations could be overcome. Computers manage information. Some of this is in the form of text, where the main requirement is storage and retrieval. A large proportion of information is numerical, with the data manipulated to provide analysis and reports.

Analogue and digital data

We use numbers to measure or to count. Measurement may have to be made of continuously varying quantities, such as pressure, acceleration, heat or time: these measurements are often difficult to define in terms of precise numbers. This type of continuously changing information is known as analogue data.

Items that can be counted are expressed in precise numbers. This is known as digital data, as literally the count could be made using the fingers of one or more hands. An abacus is a digital calculator, while a slide rule, which creates approximate answers, is an analogue device. Another good example of the difference between the two types of data can be seen in the way in which we measure time. A traditional watch, with continuously moving second, minute and hour hands presents analogue data; electronic watches use digital processors and present the same dynamic data in terms of whole numbers. Many early mathematical machines, including early calculators and computers, attempted to manage data in analogue formats, but without great success. These have now been superseded by digital machines, which convert analogue information into precise figures.

Historical development

The early seventeenth century saw many advances in the management of numbers in spite of the limitations of materials and engineering skills available at that time. Napier invented logarithms, thus endearing himself to generations of schoolboys; he also introduced a system of movable rods to perform complex calculations. This led to the development of the slide rule, which was to become the main means of mathematical calculation for more than 300 years. The need to perform complex or repetitive calculations led mathematicians such as Pascal and Liebnitz to develop calculating machines – mechanical, hand-cranked collections of toothed, metal wheels which were too complex and expensive to replace the use of slide rules.

These calculating machines, the forerunners of computers, were needed to generate speedily the long mathematical tables and ready reckoners needed by scientists, engineers and traders. The first mechanical computer was designed by Sir Charles Babbage, working in the first half of the nineteenth century. The purpose of Babbage's first machine, his 'Difference Engine', was to produce mathematical tables. Before it was finished he began to work on a never-to-be-constructed 'Analytical Engine', which would have embodied most of the components of computers as we know them today.

The Analytical Engine would have been able to store data and recall and use that data in any order; its logic mill would then process the data according to instructions given through a control unit. These instructions could be varied by entering them through a punched card, using a similar approach to controlling machinery as had been employed in the Jacquard loom. Babbage died frustrated by the inability of Victorian technology to create the machine he had designed.

Punched cards had only a limited use in calculating or managing large amounts of numbers. While they continued to have a use in managing factory machinery, their main importance was in sorting and comparing data and they were used extensively in commercial and government offices. IBM started as the result of a merger between two office supplies companies, becoming the largest supplier of punched card equipment in the world. Its involvement in this business led to its part in the development of the first major computer.

It was the emergence of the electronics industries that made possible the introduction of the first valve computers. The basic elements of a computer are simple and in theory computing devices could be made using very different approaches. For example, computers have been developed using technology based on hydraulics, but attempts such as these cannot overcome the limitations placed on speed and efficiency. Electronic computers had the advantage of not having the massive numbers of moving parts needed to operate the earlier mechanical machines.

The first valve computer was Colossus I, introduced in the UK in 1943, and used to crack the Enigma code system used by the German military command. The first US machine, ENIAC, was introduced in 1945 and used to study ballistics and calculate the trajectories of shells and bombs. Unlike Colossus, ENIAC could be used for more than one application, although reprogramming the computer was a major task. Both machines processed what were then enormous quantities of data far more efficiently than the mechanical calculators available. They were huge machines, weighing several tons and holding thousands of valves. They generated a lot of heat and were very difficult to keep running, as one burnt out valve could stop the whole machine. In spite of their size their capacity was severely limited, less than that of a hand-held computer used today. It was confidently predicted that few machines would ever be built, as few people would be able to pay for buying and running such enormous monsters.

The principles of computing are relatively straightforward and most of them had been recognised by Babbage. The machine has to have some form of input device such as a keyboard, a processor, a memory to hold the program that operates the processor, a storage of processed or unprocessed data and a means of output such as a video screen or a printer. If input and output are combined the device is known as a terminal. The operating system is also relatively simple and needs to be able to do only a few basic jobs, chiefly addition, subtraction and comparison of one value with another. In addition the system must be capable of looping, which is going around the program to perform repetitive calculations or comparisons, and also be able to branch out from one part of the program to another.

Valve computers used triodes to pass information around the system. Triodes controlled the flow of voltages and two triodes connected together formed a flip-flop circuit. The computer interpreted information by reading an 'on' or an 'off' signal generated by the position of the flip-flop circuit. This led to the use of binary mathematics, which uses 0 and 1 to operate calculations, with a complementary notation to denote letters, numbers or other characters in the operating system. Each character is represented as a combination of 0s and 1s, 0 representing 'off' and 1 'on'.

With the invention of transistors, valves were replaced with solid-state electronics. This brought down the size and cost of computers, as well as greatly improving their reliability. Transistors are sandwiches of semiconducting materials that perform the same function as valves, but without filaments that burn out. Transistors were introduced in 1948 and the first transistorised computer was produced in 1956. The next stage was to cut down the wiring which linked the transistors, partly for tidiness, but also to reduce heat and to speed up the movement of electronic signals through the computer. Transistors were mounted on boards, which also held the wiring, to make maintenance easier.

These circuits were made smaller and smaller and packed closer and closer. In present-day technology transistors and wiring have been replaced by miniaturised, extremely complex circuits etched on to small pieces of silicon, the silicon chips that we are so familiar with today. The first chips were introduced in 1969: on a 3 by 4 mm piece of silicon were packed 2,250 transistors capable of handling 100,000 activities a second. Three of these chips are the essentials of a complete computer system. Modern chips pack 250,000 circuits into the same area. Light waves are too coarse to produce these microcircuits and X-rays are used to etch the patterns on to the surface of these advanced chips. Large chips, containing millions of transistors, have been developed, but without another change in technology the limits of miniaturisation will soon be reached. The generation of heat and the distance between one part of the chip and another, even when measured in minute fractions of an inch, are limiting factors in the speed and efficiency of modern computers.

The power and cheapness of these tiny circuits have enabled the development of a wide range of new machines. We take most of these new applications for granted as they appear around us. Forty years ago there were no computers: the first to be used commercially was purchased in 1956. Twenty years ago office calculators were heavy metal machines, with hand-wound crankshafts turning cogs and wheels to perform basic arithmetic. At incredible expense in present-day terms, electric rather than electronic calculators performed the manual function and printed out a narrow paper list of the data entered and the calculation performed. Ten years ago word processors were complicated, temperamental machines using magnetic cards. Today computers that are far more powerful than those available in 1956 sit on desk tops, calculators that solve preprogrammed, complex mathematical equations are cheap, small and plentiful and word processors are used not only to make typing more efficient, but also as part of the communications network of a company.

CHAPTER 3

Basic principles and terms of computer technology

Computers come in many sizes. Mainframes are large, sometimes huge, systems either used for major tasks, such as sending satellites into outer space, or the management of the large amounts of financial information needed in the book-keeping of a company. Minicomputers are scaled-down mainframes used to satisfy the total computing needs of a smaller company or to perform large tasks in conjunction with a mainframe. Microcomputers are small computers which can sit on desk tops.

Information control and storage

The heart of the computer is its CPU, the central processing unit: it controls the passage of information, performs the logic of the program and has local memory to facilitate these activities. A small mainframe can manage between 2 and 3 million arithmetical calculations every second. With such great speed, most calculations can be performed at the most basic levels of addition or subtraction. Logic, based mainly on comparison, is used to manage text as opposed to numbers.

Memory is held in RAMs, random access memory or read-write chips, or ROMs, read only memory chips. With RAMs memory is stored at particular addresses that the CPU can seek out immediately: the information is only used to perform the task in hand and is lost if the computer is switched off. ROMs hold essential instructions to manage the operating system or to perform specific tasks. ROMs cannot be changed in any way. The programs in the ROMs are known as firmware and are part of the fabric of the machine. Where flexibility is needed programmable ROMs (PROMs or EPROMs) can be used.

Storage of information outside the CPU can be effected by using tapes, hard discs or floppy discs, held on tape or disc drives. Tapes are usually used to manage large quantities of data: most smaller business applications can be managed on hard discs or floppy discs, so-called because they are made from flexible plastic. Tapes and discs hold magnetic information and their drives act in a similar way to a tape recorder or a record player, except, in the case of discs, the records can be used for recording on as well as for playing back. Information can be held as programs, which the computer reads and holds in its core memory, or as data which the computer reads as it needs to in compliance with the instructions of the program. The computer can be set up to access simultaneously several programs or files of data held on several different tapes or discs. These storage systems require elaborate programs to manage them.

Bits, bytes and other terms

We have seen that information is stored in binary codes, which are arbitrary and can differ from computer to computer, although in practice they are very similar. Binary codes are represented by only two numbers, 0 and 1; each piece of code is known as a bit, short for binary digit, and eight bits are known as a byte, used to measure computer capacity. The number of bits that the computer can handle in any one moment is a word; mainframes have words up to 64 bits long, while micros usually can only handle eight bits. Storage of information is measured in kilobytes(K), each holding 1,024 bytes, and core memory is expressed in these terms. A typical microcomputer has 64K of core memory and a disc drive which holds a small floppy disc with a further 250K of storable information. Eight bits to a byte determine the physical abilities of the micro. The highest eight-digit binary number, 11111111, is 255, the total number of symbols that the computer can easily handle. Most computers use ASCII codes, an agreed standard for the letters and symbols generated by the machine. Each byte represents a character, so that a 64K capacity represents 64 × 1,024, or 65,536 characters.

Languages

As we saw, the computer only recognises simple electronic pulses, ons and offs, that are passed to it in very low level languages in the form of machine code. These languages are tedious and difficult to write. To make programming easier, higher level languages are used, with instructions which effectively pass through a built-in program which translates them into the low level language the computer understands. The closer the language is to human thought the less efficient will be the program in terms of speed or storage requirements. The sheer speed of the computer means that this may not be important in many applications and high level languages have opened up the use of computers to a new generation of part-time programmers.

The most widely used higher level languages are shown in Table 3.1.

Each language may have several dialects and in addition the words used even for the same dialect will change, sometimes significantly, between one type of machine and another. This is partly to use the particular machine more efficiently, but more importantly to keep customers who have invested heavily in software tied to that manufacturer.

Microcomputers can understand a wide range of programming languages. Programming the high level languages is relatively easy to learn, but difficult to master. It is worth persevering, as even a minor involvement in programming results in a clearer understanding of the strengths and weaknesses of the computer being used, an important factor when evaluating the performance of programmers.

The simplest programming language to learn is BASIC, which has several advantages over other languages. It is written in a language close to English; the program does not need to be compiled, so that it can be made to run before

Table 3.1 Most widely used higher level languages

Language	Special features	Main uses
ALGOL (ALGOrithmic Language)	Scientific language	Mathematics
APL (A Programming Language)	Very powerful in terms of expressing complex problems	Science and mathematics
BASIC (Beginner's All-purpose Symbolic Instruction Code)	Easy to learn, but not very efficient	Microcomputers and home computing
C	Powerful language designed to minimise run time and memory usage	Used for operating systems
COBOL (COmmon Business Oriented Language)	Uses simple instructions, but limited numerical capability	Widely used in business applications, such as payrolls
FORTRAN (FORmula TRANslator)	Good with mathematical expressions, but poor in handling of words	Widely used in dealing with engineering and technical problems
LISP (LISt Processing)	Data handled in the form of lists	Used by technicians to create new languages and develop artificial intelligence
LOGO	Provides easy interaction with the computer	Used in education
Pascal (named after the mathematician)	Structured, high level language	General purpose
PL/1 (Programming Language 1)	Combines features of FORTRAN and COBOL	Used for complex business programs

it has been finished to see how it looks; and it is widely understood by all levels of programmers. Its disadvantage is that its user friendliness encourages sloppy programming, making changes difficult to implement by anyone other than the original programmer – programs often never get properly debugged. A structured language such as Pascal is more difficult to learn and use, but its programs are much more secure than those written in BASIC. BASIC, however, is a powerful language and more than capable of handling most business problems.

Operating systems

Computers have one or more programs built into them or set up before the language selected can be run. These programs form the operating system and set the framework in which the program can be interpreted and applied. To make software portable from one type of computer to another the operating systems are becoming more compatible, so that changes needed to make software usable on a wide range of computers can be minimised. The ability of a microcomputer to run different operating systems is important in ensuring access to a wide range of software and preserving flexibility in the fast-changing development of small computers.

Originally, if you bought a computer you were tied to its operating system until you changed to another machine. The best-selling micros, such as Apple and Tandy, followed this tradition and came out with their own operating systems, Apple DOS (Disk Operating System) and TRS-DOS, respectively. Other suppliers had their own systems. Tandy even had different systems for different machines and found it could not transfer software from one of its own computers to later models. The DOS is a permanent resident in the computer and manages the flow of data from the program being run. It provides several utilities, allowing speedy management of data files, discs and disc drives.

The main suppliers of operating systems are two US companies called Microsoft and Digital Research. Microsoft supplies MS-DOS, and IBM uses a version of MS-DOS, PC-DOS on its personal computer. Digital Research provides a system known as CP/M (Control Program for Microcomputers), which has been the most widely used operating system up to now. Nearly 1 million CP/M systems have been sold and CP/M has the widest range of software packages written for it. To ensure that their buyers have access to this software most manufacturers will enable CP/M to be run on their machines. To convert an Apple, for example, a special board can be added to the hardware of the micro.

Other operating systems are available. The most significant for the future is Unix, developed by Bell Telephone, who are also responsible for the language C, which was used to write Unix. Unix and C could become the standard for future 16-bit microcomputers, as Unix offers a portable operating system which could be used on a wide variety of machines.

Programming

Instructions can be given to the computer directly or through programs, which can be recalled from the computer's memory. Programs can be stored on disc or tape and replanted quickly in the computer's core memory at any time in the future. The program is entered as lines of code, with line numbers to indicate the address of each particular instruction. A simple program in BASIC is shown in Fig. 3.1.

```
100 CLS
110 LOCATE 5,20:INPUT "ENTER YOUR NAME";A$
130 LOCATE 7,20:PRINT "THANK YOU ";A$
150 FOR T= 10 TO 19
160 LOCATE T,20
170 PRINT A$
180 NEXT
200 END
```

Fig. 3.1   Sample program 1

The program in Fig. 3.1 will instruct an IBM-PC to ask the operator for his name, and then will print it ten times on the screen. The first instruction is on line 100 and clears the screen of anything that may be written on it. The screen is a matrix of 25 horizontal lines by 40 vertical columns. LOCATE places output or the cursor in a particular place on the screen by defining the row and column required. The instruction on line 110 asks for the operator to enter his name, to be held in an array A$, an arrangement of data, which the computer will remember until it is switched off. Line 130 prints 'THANK YOU; A$' two lines below the original question. Line 150 is the start of a loop, which will continue until a variable, T, reaches 19, by the program looping from 10 to 19.

On line 160, T will be determined by the number of the present loop and this will LOCATE the printed message at T,20, so that each time the name A$ is printed by line 170 it will appear just below the previous printing. Line 180 completes the loop: when T equals 19 the NEXT is ignored and the program falls through to the final END.

Branching can be achieved through either of two commands, GOTO or the rather more elegant GOSUB . . . RETURN. GOTO followed by a line number sends the program to the line specified. GOSUB followed by the line number has the same result, but when the subprogram is completed, the RETURN sends the computer back to the next line or instruction after the original GOSUB command. Let us try another simple program (see Fig. 3.2). We have up to 100 sets of three numbers and we want to add up the three numbers to get the total value for each set, and the total for all the sets.

```
100  T=1:SUM=0
200  DIM A(100):DIM B(100):DIM C(100)
300  CLS:R=1
400  GOSUB 2000
500  CLS
600  IF T>100 THEN LOCATE 23,20:PRINT "YOU HAVE USED UP ALL AVAILABLE
     ENTRIES":FOR X = 1 TO 400:NEXT:GOTO 900
700  LOCATE 23,20:INPUT "DO YOU WANT TO ENTER MORE VALUES ";A$
800  IF A$="Y" THEN GOTO 300
900  CLS:R=0
1000 FOR R = 1 TO (T-1)
1100 PRINT "ENTRY NUMBER ";R;" ";A(R);"+";B(R);"+";C(R)" = ";A(R)
     +B(R)+C(R)
1200 SUM=SUM+A(R)+B(R)+C(R)
1300 NEXT
1400 PRINT "TOTAL OF ALL ENTRIES = ";SUM
1500 END
2000 LOCATE 5,10:PRINT "ENTRY NUMBER ";T:R=T
2100 LOCATE 15,20:INPUT "ENTER A";A(R)
2200 LOCATE 17,20:INPUT "ENTER B";B(R)
2300 LOCATE 19,20:INPUT "ENTER C";C(R)
2400 LOCATE 21,20: PRINT "TOTAL = ";A(R)+B(R)+C(R):T=T+1
2500 RETURN
```

Fig. 3.2 Sample program 2

Line 100 sets a variable T to 1 and a variable SUM to zero. We shall use T to distinguish one set of numbers from another and SUM to calculate the total value of all the sets added together. Line 200 tells the program to accept up to 100 different numerical values for three new variables, A, B and C; if these are not dimensioned then the computer would only accept up to ten different values for each variable. Line 400 sends us to a subroutine that starts on line 2000. Line 2000 tells us that we are about to enter values for A, B and C for the set numbered T; as this is the first run through the program this entry number is obviously 1. We will save the values for A, B and C in pigeon holes that we will retrieve by the reference number R. We then enter the three numbers associated with the first entry. Line 2400 gives the value for the sum of the three numbers entered and increases the value of T by 1 to set the entry number up for the next set. Line 2500 RETURNs us to line 600 which checks that we are not entering values outside the acceptable range; if we try to enter 101 values without an error check the program would crash and lose the data already entered. In this case the program stops us from going on and after a pause effected by a 'FOR . . . NEXT' loop, branches to the output part of the program. If we have not yet reached 100 entries line 700 asks if we want to put in another set of numbers; the $ indicates that the program expects a literal rather than a numerical value. If we say Y(es) we GOTO line 300 and branch through again. If we say anything else we GOTO line 900, clear the screen, and set R to the lowest possible value. We then enter a routine that prints the values for each entry, adds up the numbers in each set and keeps a running total in the variable SUM which changes each time the program runs through the 'FOR . . . NEXT' loop. At the end of the program the output would be as in Fig. 3.3.

```
ENTRY NUMBER 98 2+3+7 = 12
ENTRY NUMBER 99 22+12+8 = 42
ENTRY NUMBER 100 1+2+3 = 6
TOTAL OF ALL ENTRIES = 712
Ok
```

Fig. 3.3   Output at the end of the program

Ok signals that the program has finished and the computer is waiting for something else to do.

This is a very simple program, but it demonstrates several important principles. The computer has shown that it can hold in memory 300 different variables and can recall them and manipulate them to create the data ordered in the program. The value of the program increases with the number of times we will need to perform this calculation; if this is a one-off calculation it would have been quicker to do it on a calculator. However, we may have wanted to perform several calculations with the same data, sort the data into some form of ranking or use them to compare with other data we may have. We may want to save the output for a later time, in which case we could write the data to tape or disc. In these circumstances the computer really comes into its own.

The few instructions used above cover most of the logic instructions needed to program. The rest of the programming language is concerned with making the program run smoothly, error trapping, screen layout and screen handling, memory handling and printing hard copy. These requirements are not trivial and the programmer needs skill and experience to produce an efficient trouble-free program that is well documented and can be amended or enhanced at a later date without great difficulty.

The essentials of a computer are relatively easy to understand and this comparative simplicity explains the speed at which the technology of computers has been able to change and the continuing acceleration of that rate of change. The development of small, but very powerful, computer systems brings the purchasing decision down to the level of quite junior managers and this need no longer be the private preserve of a data processing manager. Consequently, there needs to be a reasonable understanding of the types of computers available and the companies that supply them and these topics are reviewed in the next chapter.

CHAPTER 4

Computers and the computer industry

Mainframes

The first growth of use of computers in business came in the 1960s with major corporations buying what are now termed mainframe computers. These companies made significant investments in equipment designed to handle major tasks or to process large amounts of data. The cost and inflexibility of these computers were such that it was often easier to reorganise the company around the computer rather than change the computer to meet individual requirements. Computers were used in financial management to produce invoices and to record receipts and payments of money, including payrolls, and thus create the book-keeping of the company. Mainframe computers require special facilities such as controlled atmosphere and temperature conditions. These special rooms house a multitude of electronic equipment stored in metal cabinets. In addition to the processor itself, tape drives for holding and retrieving data and work stations for the input and output of programs are necessary. Several people are needed to operate and maintain the equipment.

Initially, mainframes could only handle one program at a time, and data could only be accepted in batches while the computer was not processing information. As computing capacity increased these problems in using computers were solved. Mainframes became too big and powerful for all but the largest companies or applications and the machines were shared by placing terminals in remote sites. The computer's response is so fast that several users can be accommodated at the same time and the presentation of information can be made in such a way as to convince the user that he has sole use of the whole machine. Data input could be entered either by batching up work or in real time as the work arose or by a combination of the two methods.

The market for mainframes was dominated by suppliers who could invest heavily in the developing technology. IBM rose through shrewd marketing and product reliability to become the leading computer company in the world, with the financial success expected from such a position. At a time when most countries would have had problems finding such a sum, IBM could afford to invest US $5 billion in perfecting the system 360 range of computers that remains one of the most significant developments in the history of data processing. By 1960, IBM had 60 per cent of the world market for computers, as well as substantial shares of the market for typewriters and office equipment.

IBM had no serious competitors in terms of its international and product spread. It rented rather than sold its computers and rarely cut its prices. Whole industries relied on IBM, making plug-compatible hardware that undercut IBM's own equipment, often to IBM's intense annoyance. Other mainframe suppliers were forced to find special market niches or were heavily subsidised by governments concerned to ensure control over products of such strategic importance.

Minicomputers

However, not everyone needs a mainframe. To gain access to data processing smaller companies shared facilities through time-sharing arrangements with computer bureaux. Time-sharing was severely limited by the performance of the telephone systems, which were the most convenient way for carrying data to and fro. This need was satisfied by reducing the size of computers and the use of data processing became more widespread with the introduction of mini-computers. Minicomputers were the outcome of the advances in chip technology and are compact mainframes scaled down in terms of size and capacity to meet the requirements of smaller applications. Minicomputers are very powerful systems, each capable of managing a large number of terminals. As the use of computers grew, the larger companies used the minicomputers to manage front-end systems before passing data to mainframes.

IBM took a long time to respond to this development and this allowed the growth of a new tier of smaller manufacturers to take place. Digital Equipment Corporation, DEC, one of the pioneers of minicomputers, is now the second largest producer of computers after IBM. This development arose because IBM had underestimated market needs and because it faced major anti-trust suits, of a scale that threatened to employ armies of lawyers full-time for generations. Many of these suits had been caused by IBM's past use of its strength to ensure its continuing market domination. These factors combined to reduce IBM's market share to 40 per cent by 1980.

Recent growth and market share of large companies

It is worth putting the industry in perspective. The largest companies are shown in Table 4.1; the recent growth of some companies, such as Apple, has been very rapid.

Table 4.1 shows what a dominant company IBM is; it has enjoyed this position since the 1960s, when IBM and other industry leaders were known to Wall Street analysts as 'Snow White and the Seven Dwarfs', a relationship IBM has been very careful to preserve. This dominance is shown by the extra-ordinary effect single decisions by the company have on the whole industry. The 360 range of computers that was introduced in the 1960s and which established IBM's market dominance brought with it the concept of an operating system – before that all programs had to operate the computer and interact with any other program directly, making software extremely difficult to write. Then in 1969 IBM decided to unbundle its products and market hard-ware and software separately. Whole new industries appeared, providing

Table 4.1 Largest computer and office equipment companies in 1983

Rank	Company	Country	Sales ($ millions)	Profits ($ millions)
1	IBM	US	40,180	5,485
2	Philips	Netherlands	16,177	227
3	Siemens	West Germany	15,724	297
4	Honeywell	US	5,753	231
5	Sperry	US	5,076	118
6	Hewlett Packard	US	4,710	432
7	Control Data	US	4,583	162
8	Texas Instruments	US	4,580	(145)
9	Burroughs	US	4,297	197
10	DEC	US	4,272	284
11	Fujitsu	Japan	3,834	193
12	NCR	US	3,731	288
13	Olivetti	Italy	2,458	194
14	Ricoh	Japan	1,561	40
15	Wang	US	1,538	152
16	Bull	France	1,527	(82)
17	ICL	UK	1,321	60
18	Nixdorf	West Germany	1,062	35
19	Apple	US	983	77
20	Data General	US	829	55

Source: Fortune 500

IBM-compatible hardware and software products. A decision to sell rather than just rent equipment created a new demand for leasing facilities from banks and the formation of new finance companies.

The move into microcomputers, with the IBM-PC, has been just as dramatic, and the appearance of what should become the standard operating system in that confused market will make life much easier for communications and networking. Equally significant has been a new willingness to work with companies outside the IBM network, such as retailers (to sell the personal computers) and software companies, and to work in an area in which IBM is lagging technologically, office telecommunications.

IBM also has an impact on the computer market whenever it buys parts for itself. IBM is one of the largest producers of chips in the world, all of its production being used internally. When IBM had to buy chips in the market during 1982 it created a major shortage that seriously affected other producers. IBM's PC also caused problems for competitors, as its success created delays in supplying disc drives to other manufacturers, who, like IBM, assemble their microcomputers from bought-in parts.

IBM's product range is extensive. While it is now doing something to fill the gap in its range at the lower price levels, one area that it withdrew from is at the top end, the supercomputer that is used for very large, specialised tasks. It is here that the Japanese, long considered the main threat to US manufacturers, are investing heavily. Supercomputers can process astonishing amounts of data, currently at a rate of 300 million operations a second; by 1990 Cray Research, the leading manufacturer of supercomputers, hopes to have a machine capable of handling 10,000 million transactions a second, using technology that is still being developed. Supercomputer technology is the basis for much innovation in computer development, particularly research in computer intelligence. At some time, no doubt, IBM will re-enter this market, but probably only if it feels its larger mainframe business is under attack.

If IBM has to look over its shoulder, a major concern it may have is the looming shape of AT & T, the largest telephone company in the world. The ways in which we use telephones will change dramatically now computers and microprocessors can be placed at the heart of the telephone exchange. It is not too fanciful to envision the worldwide telephone network as an enormous computer neatly held together with data lines, which will become more and more efficient as new technology replaces the existing exchanges.

Microcomputers

As computers came down in size they became more robust and easier to program. The operations of a computer are managed by microprocessors, large-capacity chips, which can be mass-produced cheaply. The difference between the microprocessor used in a washing machine and one used in a computer is that the latter is programmable. Microprocessors are now so powerful they can be used to operate a complete computer system, making generally available the microcomputers that are sold in High Street shops and designed for consumers from the age of 5 upwards. Microcomputers have evolved quickly to become serious business machines with an important place in the office of the future. Micros provide intelligent terminals with their own computing capacity to analyse data taken from much more powerful host computers, enabling work to be performed to meet individual requirements. The ability to manage these terminals to obtain optimum use of their capabilities will be an important skill.

Microcomputers are entering their fourth generation, having evolved through 4-bit, 8-bit, 16-bit and now 32-bit processors, which are just coming off the drawing board. The prospect of a desk-top computer, as powerful as a mini, capable of handling 1 million instructions a second and as easy to use as a television set, is not very far away.

Microcomputer systems will become more and more important as they increase in power with the rapid advances being made in both chip technology and memory capacity. The first microcomputers were marketed in the late 1970s, towards the end of a consumer revolution brought about by the mass production of low-priced electronic chips. The first of these chips were used in calculators and digital watches; as chips grew larger they were used in the video game machines which replaced traditional coin-in-the-slot machines in pubs and amusement arcades.

Video games came of age with the Japanese-inspired Space Invaders, which became so popular in Japan that the coins needed to play the machines were often in short supply. Video games were the first introduction many people had to the capabilities of the new microprocessors and this early success led to two developments. The first was an explosion of new games and games machines which took place in 1981 and 1982. The second was less obvious and started earlier. This was the use of similar chips to make home computers.

There is no obvious use for a computer in the home, unless it is to play games or for intellectual stimulation. Its practical uses are very limited unless it is wired into a control system of some sort or linked to a data base through a telephone line. However, games are more enjoyable on a purpose-built machine and control systems are more efficient using specially designed, cheaper chips. Access to a data base is needed for management of financial matters or for office work, and office work that has been brought home is the likely use that the larger microcomputers will be put to. The true home computer will be used mostly as an educational device, preparing our children for the computer age in which they will live as they grow up.

The first home computers were marketed by Apple and by Tandy. In the UK today it is possible to buy any one of over 150 different models from over 100 different manufacturers. The market splits into two components, the cheaper end for home use and the more expensive side for office microcomputer systems. The leading suppliers to the consumer market in the UK are Sinclair, Acorn, Commodore and the BBC. Prices start from less than £40 for a Sinclair ZX81 with 1K of RAM memory, to several thousand pounds for specialist systems, depending on the size of the machine and its peripheral equipment. The consumer market is similar to the toy market in many of its characteristics, and several suppliers, including companies such as Texas Instruments, Atari (now a subsidiary of Warner Communications) and Dragon found 1983 heavy going in terms of fierce price competition and falling profitability.

The main reason for these problems has been the entry into the market by IBM. IBM has been re-establishing its strength with the decision in the late 1970s to become a 'price aggressive' producer, a successful strategy designed to win back business from the plug-compatible competitors. The lifting of anti-trust actions in early 1982 has been swiftly followed by a new aggression in a company never noted for its docile nature. IBM became at the same time price competitive and quick to release new products, forcing competitors to guess where the price for the new products would fall by the time they could get their own competing models on the market.

In 1980 IBM decided to look at the market for personal computers, which would require breaking with some of its long-held traditions, particularly the use of independent retailers to distribute the products. As with minicomputers, IBM has followed a strategy, not of being first in the market, but of producing computers that effectively set industry standards. IBM's entry into a confused market place made microcomputers respectable, polarising it into two segments, the serious users and the hobbyists.

The stakes in the home computer business are very high. The market is very confused and it is difficult to work out the price of the equipment and which peripherals are essential and which are merely nice to have. One thing is certain, the equipment will cost much more than at first appears, once sales tax and other hidden costs are added on.

In the UK the very cheap computers have been selling very well, many through the multiple chain stores such as Boots and W. H. Smith. The American consumer has been far more reluctant to buy the cheaper machines, probably because he has a higher degree of computer literacy and therefore a higher expectation than his British counterpart. One approach to overcome this reluctance is to package complete systems: the much-advertised launch of the CBS/Coleco Adam computer, delayed due to problems with software, provides, for around US $600, a system that includes a good quality printer, word processing, high speed tape memory and the ability to take games cartridges.

Advertising budgets are huge, particularly in the US, mostly pre-emptive in the need to attract buyers before IBM really gets into its stride. In the UK the quality newspapers bulge with advertisements for all types of computer equipment and the magazine racks contain dozens of titles, some covering general topics, most aimed at the owners of particular machines.

Even before IBM's intervention in the market, the home computer manufacturers were doing a pretty good job of destroying each other. Leading the charge was Texas Instruments, following a well established policy of forcing down prices against production costs predicated by assumed levels of sales. Texas Instruments hoped that this strategy would 'rationalise' the market by forcing out high cost producers: the strategy had been successful for Texas Instruments in markets for calculators, chips and digital watches. Home computers proved to be far more difficult and it came as a surprise when in the second quarter of 1983 its consumer division lost US $183 million, caused by the company's inability to shift product out of its warehouse and into the market: by the end of October 1983 Texas Instruments announced that it was withdrawing from the home computer market.

Texas Instruments was not the only company to misread the market. Most of the manufacturers of video games had been diversifying out of the toy market into the personal computer market, but were caught by the speed at which demand for video games has fallen away; this has come at a time when significant investment is needed to produce the home computers they have designed. The producers of the more expensive machines are finding it equally difficult and even the producers of machines for the business market have not been immune. Osborne, who had captured a strong niche in portable computers, has sought protection from the US courts against its creditors. Osborne sold a reasonably powerful computer, with basic software needed for most business applications factored into the price. While the computers were 'luggable' rather than truly portable they satisfied a market need: inept management and the arrival of lightweight portable computers caused the company's decline. Several other companies, such as Victor and Fortune, are struggling and even Apple has seen a major slow-down in profits as it brings its new machines to market. The industry is certainly sorting itself out.

The more expensive, larger machines have found important new markets as small business systems, in addition to supplying the upper end of the consumer market for machines used for more serious applications than playing Space Invaders.

Apple ships the most machines, but its place as market leader is being overtaken by IBM, in spite of the latter's late entry into the microcomputer markets. Another late entrant is DEC, which pioneered the development of the minicomputer as the first real alternative to the mainframe and is now a major international supplier in its own right. Apple, DEC and IBM are likely to dominate the market for small business systems for the next few years, although both Apple and DEC have seen falling profit margins due to lower than expected sales volumes following IBM's sudden rise in market share.

Apple is a young company that has already firmly established itself as a major supplier of electronic equipment. More than anyone else, Apple made the small computer acceptable and sufficiently reliable for carrying out critical tasks in office and factory use. Apple was one of the first in the market, hence its strong market share both in the US and in the UK. Apple's main machine, the Apple IIe, is a tidied up version of its original home computer, introduced in 1976. About 750,000 Apple IIes have been sold since that time. Apple's larger machine, the Apple III, has been unable to emulate the immediate success of the IIe, but has also sold well. Apple's latest products are the Lisa and its scaled down version, the MacIntosh: both are very advanced machines, with an extensive range of built-in software.

IBM has expanded its sales of personal computers very rapidly. The IBM-PC is a 16-bit machine – which means it should be about twice as fast as the eight-bit Apple IIe – with the potential to carry much more memory. IBM has introduced a variant, the IBM-PCXT, which has a built-in hard disc, giving it considerable capacity and fast memory handling.

The casualties among the home computer manufacturers will increase once IBM starts to deliver in quantity its home computer, the PC Jr, which retails for a fraction of the price of the PC, and is rumoured to be the first of a family of progressively cheaper home computers aimed at different market segments. The Jr is expensive in terms of home computers. The cheapest version uses cartridge-based programmes, while the more expensive versions have a single disc drive; most, but by no means all, of the software written for the PC will run on the more expensive versions, which are aimed clearly at the 'take work home on a disc' market. The only technological innovation is a truly floating, cordless keyboard that operates the PC Jr with an infra-red beam. IBM's initial marketing has not been very successful, and the product has had to be re-packaged, with a more businesslike keyboard and additional memory, in an attempt to emulate the success of the earlier machines.

DEC's machines have impressive specifications, but have only just been introduced to the market. DEC PCs have been developed from its mini-computer technology and the top of the range Professional is a very powerful machine.

Microcomputers are versatile, capable of working independently or acting as intelligent terminals for a mainframe or minicomputer. Microcomputers can also be linked together through networks, with the micros sharing facilities or performing special functions for the whole network. Networked micros are efficient and reliable systems for transaction processing and information management. Networked micros can provide as much power as minis or even small mainframes and there are several benefits to be gained from an approach that results in distributed processing. We shall be seeing an application of network techniques later in the book.

Buying a micro is far less fraught with financial consequences than the purchase of a mini or a mainframe. Most micros are first smuggled into companies to avoid the wrath of the data processing managers and are generally paid for out of the stationery budget. Now that IBM is in the market micros have become more acceptable and a more organised approach to their purchase should be possible.

Software available

We have been looking at the development of hardware: hardware is the physical structure of the computer and the term can be extended to cover single-purpose machines which have built-in microprocessors, such as washing machines or microwave ovens. Computers can only run by receiving instructions through programs, which are known collectively as software. While the effectiveness of software may be constrained by the hardware, good software can greatly enhance the value of the equipment. Software has an impact on the computer at several levels; writing it requires both discipline and creativity.

When it becomes necessary to employ a computer, users have the alternatives of buying software packages or commissioning especially written software to solve their problems. Off-the-shelf software is available for many financial applications, particularly accounting records, sales ledgers, and data base management, such as customer and supplier records.

Apple and IBM offer their customers one very important advantage, the existence of a very extensive and growing library of off-the-shelf programs, ranging from complete accounting packages to video games.

Word processing and document filing and retrieval are important uses of small computers. Report generation and the graphical presentation of information are provided quickly and accurately. Prices for software vary widely depending on the size of the hardware needed to handle the problem.

Many needs can be satisfied by using utility programs such as Visicalc, an electronic spreadsheet, which can claim to have been a fundamental contributor to the development of microcomputers, particularly Apples. An electronic spreadsheet holds a matrix of cross-referenced data entries. Data are entered as labels or values. Labels are used for column or row headings and for placing text in the spreadsheet. The matrix resembles a sheet of analysis paper divided into rows and columns. Values are numbers entered into a particular square that has been ruled off by the intersection of the rows and columns. Each square has a unique reference. As well as holding labels or values, squares can also hold the results of calculations, by making the values in any number of other squares interact with each other. The result of calculations can thus be used to interact with the result of other calculations, and the sophistication of the use of the spreadsheet is often constrained by the mathematical capability of the operator. Information handling is extremely simple and repetitive programming of the spreadsheet is simplified, especially the creation and storage of data files.

The true magic of a spreadsheet is the ability to change a value and see how the rest of the spreadsheet is affected by the change. Thus financial forecasts can be entered and 'what ifs' easily performed. Financial reports can be amended quickly and the effect seen instantly, with major savings in time, paper and frustration. A spreadsheet will usually pay for an office micro-computer within a few weeks.

Spreadsheets have generated new demands for data management. Visicorp, the distributors of Visicalc, has followed two strategies, the development of compatible utilities and the introduction of integrated software. Visicalc's wide usage makes it sensible to develop other utilities that can share the data files that are written for the spreadsheet program. These programs prepare graphs, larger data bases or complex financial models.

For less than £100 Visicalc in its simplest form provides a spreadsheet that can hold 63 columns and 256 rows, over 16,000 pieces of information. Newer spreadsheets have concentrated on trying to make the spreadsheet more user friendly, but until recently have not made much impression in Visicalc's market strength. Trends in software are away from single-application programs. A spreadsheet-based package aimed at IBM-PCs called Lotus 123 has proved very successful. It is made up of three elements, a powerful spreadsheet, a graphics package and a database manager, and has good text handling features. All these facilities are integrated, with the graphics working directly from the database that has been prepared from the spreadsheet. As with all integrated software, Lotus requires a considerable amount of memory.

Lotus 123 is a stepping stone to the next generation of packaged software. The evolution started with the work done by Xerox Corporation in the US, which resulted in a system called Smalltalk. Xerox was developing the concept of a managerial work-station, providing the manager with all the computer support he would need built into his working environment. The result was the Xerox Star, an expensive system that had limited success, but which showed the way that software development would have to go. Smalltalk used an interactive screen, easy movement between built-in software programs and a concept of screen and program handling based on a mouse, a small box on a roller, which when moved across a desk moves a cursor around the computer's screen.

The Apple Lisa is a far cheaper version of the Star. It is a complex machine capable of carrying out two or more tasks at the same time. A considerable amount of core and disc memory storage, both hard and floppy, is provided. The integrated software covers a suite of programs – Lisacalc, Lisawrite, etc. – for spreadsheets, word processing, graphics, drawing, network planning and data base management. These programs are interactive and output from one can be used as input for another. The screen looks like a normal piece of paper, with black text on a white background. When the Lisa is switched on, its display shows a stylised depiction of an office desk top, on which various files and utilities are represented by symbols. By selecting a symbol with the mouse, the contents of a file or the blank work sheet of a utility come up on the screen. Several of these can be opened at the same time and activated by the movement of the mouse.

Screen handling is quite startling, with pieces of electronic paper going in and out of files by clicks on the mouse. The screen is bit-mapped, showing text and pictures in exactly the way they will be printed. Anything on the screen can be moved around easily and graphical displays can be reduced in size or enlarged to a size that could be several times bigger than the size of the screen itself. By switching from a spreadsheet to a graphics worksheet the numbers on the spreadsheet are immediately displayed on a line, bar, scatter or pie chart (a feature of the Lotus 123 package). A change of numbers on the spreadsheet immediately changes the graph. The titles and headings can be moved freely around the graph in a multitude of typefaces and typesizes. The graph can be 'cut out' and 'pasted' on to an electronic clipboard, then transferred to a report prepared on the word processing program, and inserted in the text. The electronic work space even includes a wastepaper basket in which junk items can be thrown and retrieved if wanted later on by rummaging through the waste paper.

The Lisa is designed to be usable by a novice within a matter of a few hours. Each program package comes with extensive documentation and, as with any package, experience will greatly increase their usefulness. It is also a fully functioning computer capable of running most languages. The Lisa does not cost much more than any other large micro by the time the extra memory and associated hardware has been paid for. The library of software comes at a very reasonable price. Lisa's manufacturers have aimed fairly and squarely at the business market, rather than the home user.

Apple's marketing of the Lisa has not been very effective and has suffered from the outstanding success of the IBM-PC. A cheaper, scaled down version, the MacIntosh, has been introduced with many of the features of the Lisa, although the software has been unbundled from the hardware. The MacIntosh comes with a mouse and is operated in much the same way as the Lisa. The software, MacWrite and MacPaint, is not as integrated as that on the Lisa, but provide very effective word processing and graphics capabilities. The Lisa and the MacIntosh set new standards in user friendliness and software capability.

The MacIntosh, like the IBM PC-Jr, suffers from having too little available memory for the serious business user. Memory is now a critical factor as the new integrated software needs considerable space just to run, and is capable of creating very large databases and stored output very quickly. Symphony, the enhanced version of Lotus 123, which adds integrated word processing and communications capabilities to the spreadsheet, graphics and database facilities of the earlier program, is an example of a software package whose potential can only be realised with considerably more memory than is currently available on most microcomputers. IBM will probably concentrate more on larger capacity machines, and its keenly priced range of PC-AT (Advanced Technology) computers, introduced in 1984, provide ample memory on line and on hard discs, Xenix (IBM's version of the Unix operating system) and networking facilities.

Programmers

Programmers fall into three types. First, most large companies have programmers for their mainframe who may be freed to provide the service that the treasurer needs. The key factors will be the length of time that this will take to be completed and the priority the program will receive on the mainframe once it is tested and ready to run. Secondly, there may be programmers who work directly for the treasurer. Here the problems are probably to do with training. The programmer is isolated from people who work on the same sorts of problem and is likely to need a lot of off-the-job training to keep him up-to-date and motivated. Thirdly, there are consultants, who fall into two main categories, systems designers and code writers: the former are much more expensive than the latter.

The key to managing programmers is to specify clearly what is wanted and review on a very regular basis how the work is progressing, so that you are certain that the programmer is producing exactly what is wanted and any compromises are made with full agreement on both sides. Programmers are like foreign exchange dealers. Much of their work is humdrum and repetitive, but requires a person with a flair akin to artistic talent to get the best results. As with dealers they need special care and handling.

If programmers seem a 'rum lot', they are at least well meaning (although if they are consultants, they will always find ways to charge just a little more). Buying a small computer is a certain way to meet unknowledgeable salesmen who certainly do not have your interest at heart, but would like you to buy an expensive bundle of boxes and cables (as long as you don't ask them too many questions about how it works). Once you have been through the handbooks you will know considerably more about the computers than the salesmen do. A small business system costs around £100,000, sufficient to cripple a small company if it does not perform; sooner or later a large treasury will need a small business system of its own to run in parallel with the company's mainframe.

Commissioning software

Using packaged software will inevitably require a compromise between the general requirements of the market that the software was aimed at and the specific needs of the user. If off-the-shelf software has to be adapted to meet specific requirements, the degree of change needed will make a major difference to the cost. It may be preferable to commission software, either from in-house data processing specialists or from outside consultants.

In-house specialists tend to think in terms of mainframes and are not used to delivering software quickly. Priorities are set and changed depending on rather obscure bureaucratic principles, apparently designed to ensure that the end user is not consulted. Unless the requirement is for a standard procedure, it is often difficult to find a programmer who can understand the problem that has to be solved. This is not a complaint, but an observation: in-house programmers have to satisfy the needs of their most important and largest users first and have little time to be sidetracked into the specialised needs of a company, such as the oddities of treasury management.

External consultants can be just as difficult and frustrating to work with, but then at least the user has only himself to blame if he pays for bad work. The main problem with consultants is getting them to deliver on time. Thereafter, particularly with complex programs, you have to rely on the consultant, and the importance he places on you as a client, to have your software maintained or enhanced. More importantly, the choice of hardware may be determined by the consultant's background. Consultants can only be judged by the work that they do, which should be tightly specified and that specification only changed once both parties have agreed on the impact of that change in terms of delivery time and cost.

An alternative is to write programs yourself or employ one of the growing number of 'computer literates' coming out of schools and universities who can write excellent programs quickly. A side benefit will be the supply of games needed to keep up morale, both of the programmer and those who wait (sometimes a bit longer than they expected to) for the fruits of his labours.

The computer industry is thus made up of two main components, the manufacturers of hardware and the writers of software. Good software can often overcome the deficiencies of the hardware. In general, the larger the computer the higher the profit for the manufacturers, who find the retail market for home computers difficult to manage, as the profit per unit is minute compared with that of larger systems. An element of growing importance is the ability to transmit data from one computer to another, often over long distances, and communications have now become the third major plank of modern business technology.

CHAPTER 5

Communications

The development of international trading has increased the need to move information quickly over long distances. The evolution through mail, telegraph, telephone and telex has taken about 100 years. The pace of change has been very rapid. With the telephone, for example, it takes so long to replace equipment that whole new systems are obsolescent by the time that they are installed. The capital cost and the work involved in replacing old systems means that many places continue to use old equipment, with operators running manual switchboards side by side with the most up-to-date automatic exchanges. The next ten years will see changes take place at an even more rapid pace.

The first means of fast transmission of written messages was the telegram, or cable, often the most efficient form of communication when compared to early telephone services. Telex (an abbreviation of telegraph exchange) is a system of sending and receiving messages over the telegraph exchange, using terminals in the sender's and receiver's offices. It is a conversational medium and is widely used in financial institutions, as it provides written evidence of a conversation or instruction which can be authenticated by a test word, a pre-arranged code between the two parties indicating that the message has been sent by an authorised person. Telex terminals are becoming more sophisticated, with video screens and built-in word processing facilities. The telex network is used by over 1 million subscribers and new refinements are continuously being made with the objective of automating it further and improving the speed of transmission of the signal. Telex was the forerunner of electronic mail and was an important ingredient in the mix of communication devices.

Centralisation of information flows

Early communication systems established the basic rules for the management of flows of information. Letters are collected in a central sorting office for efficient redistribution rather than carried from the sender straight to their final destination. Sorting offices send packages of mail to other sorting offices who split up the packages and send the letters and parcels to the intended recipient. The concept of a clearing centre can be used to make any flows of information between several points more efficient.

Telephone communications

Telephones follow the same centralised approach; it would be impractical to lay lines directly to all the people that we would want to speak to, so lines go into a central point and there are connected up to the designated receiver. Centralisation of information flows invariably means better controls over the physical distribution of those flows and quicker routing of calls.

All telephone lines go through a central exchange; initially exchanges were manned by one or more switchboard operators. These people had the power to hear everything that was going on, to circulate gossip and to give advice on matters of commercial importance. In the late nineteenth century, in a small American town, the competition between two undertakers was being swung in the favour of the business run by the husband of the local switchboard operator. This so infuriated the other undertaker, Almon Strowger, that he invented a mechanical relay that became the basis for the first automatic telephone exchanges. Strowger exchanges use rotary switches that make electromagnetic connections to generate the number being dialled. The next development, around 1930, was to speed up the process using crossbar exchanges, which reduced the number of switches to a single metal bar connecting the two parties of the call. The crossbar approach is the basis for electronic exchanges which have the advantage of having no moving parts. The features of the crossbar are now part of computer programs that make up SPC (stored program control) exchanges. These offer electronic facilities that automatically monitor usage by subscribers and provide flexibility in changing the configuration of the exchange without the need of physical intervention by an engineer.

The computer that sits at the heart of an electronic exchange monitors the signals being sent to it, decides the best way to connect incoming calls to the intended receiver and manages the transmission of messages over the network. Signalling starts when the handset is picked up and the exchange responds with its own signal, the dialling tone. A series of signals, the telephone number, connect the caller to either a ringing or an engaged tone. If the call is successfully connected then the exchange monitors a signal showing that the ringing tone has stopped and then picks up a clear signal when the handset is replaced on its hook. A telephone exchange is therefore a burble of tones received or sent out by the controlling computer system.

Computerisation means better utilities for users. Many people are familiar with the computerised telephone equipment used in offices, which has digital equipment in its PABX, Private Automatic Branch Exchanges. PABX have several features to help the subscriber, including abbreviated dialling, redialling busy numbers, diverting calls, stopping calls from coming through, holding calls until the line is free, automatic alarm call and telephone conference facilities. IBM has a system, ADS, which enables callers to leave recorded messages for busy extensions, rather than having to keep redialling engaged extensions. One day all these will be standard features on home telephones. In the UK a ten-year project which started in 1980 will see the whole telephone system replaced with computerised exchanges, capable of providing these services, to ensure a creditable performance for the UK within the context of an increasingly sophisticated worldwide telephone network.

Telephone lines are now used for voice and data transmission and facsimile transmission of documents. The speed at which data can be moved from one place to another is measured by the number of bits (each a '1' or '0') sent per second, known as the baud rate (named after Émile Baudot, an early pioneer in data transmission).

The technology of the physical transmission of messages is moving at the same rapid pace as computerisation of the exchanges. Satellites, optical fibre cables and cordless telephones are evidence of this. The significance of these changes is the ability to carry more communications lines and the increased speed and efficiency of the network, preparing the way for the greater volumes of traffic that future data transmission will bring.

Analogue and digital systems

Traditional telephone equipment uses analogue signals. As the signal travels down the telephone line it loses strength and has to be amplified through repeaters every few miles; these also amplify any interference that may have crept in. This is of less concern for voice communication than for data transmission. On a digital system all transmission, voice and data, is broken down into binary code and the repeaters merely read and retransmit the code rather than boosting it through amplifiers. Noise is therefore eliminated.

The most significant technological changes will come from the replacement of present-day public exchanges with digital switching equipment. This will permit the efficient transmission of computer-originated material. As mentioned earlier, present telephone lines can only carry analogue signals; computer traffic has first to be converted from binary, or digital, signals, using a modem (a modulator/demodulator). Modems can send information at 200 baud, a constraint for computers capable of communicating in terms of millions of bits per second. Transmission speeds are unacceptably slow for most data processing requirements and interference on the line can result in garbled messages. These problems are mollified by plumbing the modems into private, leased lines and efficiently using the data lines through multiplexing, which is the simultaneous transmission of several different pieces of data at the same time. The multiplexer receives the data and passes them to the modem in a jumbled form and the information is unjumbled by a multiplexer at the other end.

Packet switching, the ability to break down messages into parts and later reconstituting them into their original form, is an important part of modern communications, as it means that messages can be sent by the shortest or cheapest route. With voice or analogue signals, multiplexers separate the various messages into different frequencies within the same waveband being used on the telephone line. Packet switching networks are available through British Telecom, although there are capacity problems, as demand has been far greater than present equipment can support. This type of communication has been controlled around the world for the most part by the government bodies responsible for the mail and telephones; in the US it has been developed by private businesses such as Telenet and Tymnet.

Digital switching equipment will translate voices into digital signals and voice or data is transmitted in pieces that are sent on different circuits and re-assembled at the other end, using synchronisation signals tagged on to each element of the message. By 1990 most telephone exchanges around the world will be using digital systems, reflecting the growing importance of data transmission. Not only will data be split through multiplexing, they will also be split into packets and the packets sent out over the network through any available channel. The digital networks will enable much greater ease in connecting, for example, a machine which reads the information held on a credit card directly to the computer which holds details of the relevant bank account or charge account, without the need for human intervention. The establishment of a common, but widely distributed, data base, accessed through a terminal (probably a microcomputer) on the manager's desk will be a feature of the office of the future, made possible by the new telephone exchanges.

Developments in the market

Allowing the introduction of new technology to take its own course may be the best strategy in a fast-changing environment. Much of this change will come as a result of the struggle for market dominance that is looming between the two great monoliths of the technology business. AT & T and IBM are squaring up to each other, each threatening to enter the other's market. Symbolically their buildings are side by side in New York, as if the two giant corporations were glaring at each other through their towering glass walls. AT & T is making important strides towards developing computer-based activities that many observers see as leading directly into confrontation with IBM, the first time a corporation with comparable financial muscle has appeared to threaten IBM's traditional stronghold for many years. IBM is investing significantly in communications technology with joint ventures in satellite and PABX developments. IBM is a secretive company, but its widespread geographical presence makes it a name that is familiar to most people. AT & T has been confined to the US market and so is less well known.

The development of communications in the US took a significant turn in the 1920's when Western Electric, a part of AT & T – American Telephone and Telegraph – split off its international business to prevent an anti-trust action in the US. AT & T was already a dominant supplier of telecommunications in the US, even at that time the largest market for such equipment. Western Electric had been making and selling equipment all around the world; the non-US business was sold to ITT – International Telephone and Telegraph – a separate company altogether. The sale of the business was accompanied by an undertaking that AT & T and ITT would not compete in each other's markets, with AT & T keeping the US, and ITT, in its own right or as agent for AT & T's exports, looking for business in the rest of the world. ITT became a major force in the world telecommunications business by taking over well established manufacturing businesses, including STC in the UK.

This cosy arrangement continues more or less to this day, although there are signs that competition between the two companies is increasing, for example, for international telephone business between the US and other countries. AT

& T has therefore had little competition on its home territory and has provided, through the Bell System, over 80 per cent of all telephone services in the US. AT & T's shares have long been considered among the safest on Wall Street and were the most heavily traded stock.

AT & T was organised very simply, with Bell Labs providing Research and Development and product design, Western Electric manufacturing the products and Bell operating companies installing and maintaining the equipment. AT & T has for many years been in conflict with the US Justice Department. To settle the anti-trust dispute 22 regional Bell companies have been spun off into seven new regional telephone holding companies. AT & T itself has restructured quickly and effectively, with the old company writing off over US $5 billion at the end of 1983, reflecting the difference between running a monopoly and a competitive business. Its new structure is made up of Western Electric (manufacturing, Bell Labs, R and D), AT & T Communications (long distance), AT & T International (overseas) and AT & T Information Systems (for domestic business). AT & T loses its 'Ma Bell' trademarks which are retained by the new holding companies, which will each be in its own right among the largest public utilities in the US.

AT & T retains the rights for long distance connections which will result in significant price increases for local services, as local calls tended to be subsidised by the long distance revenues. In almost every other respect it will be competing with its old subsidiaries and with other suppliers. The result could be a search for new markets overseas, including joint ventures such as those arranged with Phillips and Olivetti, which could lead it into more direct confrontation with ITT, or to extend its product range, to ensure it is well placed to manage the changes arising from the installation of digital communications networks.

The anti-trust case was prompted by the changes in technology that were preventing AT & T, which had been allowed to operate only in certain areas under previous legislation, from supplying the new equipment, such as computerised PABX which were being introduced by new competitors in the industry. It was part of an overall programme of deregulation that saw an end to the distinction between carriers of voice, telegraph and computer data transmissions, which under the old legislation had to be performed by different companies. In addition, companies could freely perform those services either within the US or overseas. The competition will also be sharpened by new technologies, such as microwave radio or satellites, which will enable companies to talk to each other without the need for land lines or any other intermediaries.

AT & T now has the ability to take advantage of some of its more advanced ideas. For example, it can now distribute commercially its Unix and C software, which were developed by Bell Labs, but could not be sold by the company. Both the Unix operating system and the C language could become standards for business applications using microcomputers.

These rapid changes in technology have been accompanied by other major events, including the lifting of anti-trust lawsuits against IBM in the US and the trend towards deregulation in the PTTs – postal, telephone and telegraph companies – around the world. With the continuing trend towards deregulation in the US, where legal protection for certain industries such as airlines, banking and telecommunications is being lifted, AT & T, which traditionally had been treated as if it were a PTT, has lost its protected position. Its monopoly position in providing services such as international calls has been significantly eroded. This giant company is seeking to expand its business outside the US and this will lead to pressure on the PTT monopolies in European countries. Some will feel obliged to follow the UK's lead in liberalising the telecommunications services, although it is unlikely that they will go as far as the UK Government's decision to denationalise British Telecom.

The UK Government is determined to introduce a measure of competition into the telecommunications industry. The UK has thus seen a major development in the formation of a new telecommunications company, Mercury Communications, started by a consortium made up of Barclays Bank, Cable and Wireless, and British Petroleum, to provide alternative communications to the present British Telecom services. The company is laying down a £50 million investment in an inter-city network that will interface with British Telecom's national and international connections. Aimed at large commercial users, the communication system will be made up of microwave transmission for local messages and optical fibre cables laid alongside the inter-city railway lines for long distance calls. The interaction with British Telecom is ill-defined and in some instances seems somewhat tenuous and Mercury certainly must rely on British Telecom's goodwill if it is to succeed.

Mercury has a 25-year licence to operate telecommunications services in competition with British Telecom and it enjoys a level of protection, as it is unlikely that other licences will be granted in the near future. British Telecom's response cannot be termed friendly and has included sharp price cutting in the long distance services Mercury intends to provide, as well as the introduction of digital links for commercial customers, another main plank of Mercury's strategy. With British Telecom sharpening its pencil, Mercury has been forced to reconsider its strategies, but it has a new opportunity as a result of the development of cable TV in the UK and should be able to gain a reasonable share of this business from British Telecom.

Mercury is an inevitable development given the Conservative Government's decision to sell off the shares of British Telecom to the public, which given the size of the proposed issue will create many problems, not least the need to have good trade union relationships during the sell-down of the stock. British Telecom has a market value of some £4 billion or more for the 51 per cent that the Government will be selling off. The decision has opened the way for companies such as Mercury and for competition for the supply of equipment, such as PABX.

British Telecom still has a monopoly position in certain respects, as it retains the right to vet and veto the specification of competitors' equipment to ensure compatability with its own systems. It also controls the allocation and priority of use of channels on satellites. As British Telecom remains the major customer for equipment, its main suppliers, based in the UK, are unlikely to be too aggressive in the home market and competition is likely to come from overseas suppliers. Much of that competition will be to supply British Telecom itself.

UK companies will be going out into the world to sell their own technology, principally the System X range of digital telephone exchanges, to reduce their dependence on one large buyer. British Telecom has been very slow in introducing digital exchanges and in phasing out the older equipment. As a result, the two manufacturers, GEC and Plessey, who together manufacture System X, have had little chance to build production capacity with a non-existent home market and this has seriously constrained their ability to sell the system overseas. British Telecom has threatened to place orders for digital exchanges overseas if the UK manufacturers cannot reduce delays in developing the System X equipment. These overseas competitors are formidable and include L.M. Ericsson, Northern Electric, AT & T, ITT, and the Phillips/AT & T joint venture.

British Telecom has also sped up the introduction of new services to carry digital messages. In addition to its Datel, a modem-based service, and the Packet Switching Service, a public data network, British Telecom is also rushing through three new services, MegaStream, KiloStream and Integrated Digital Access, which will raise the speed and efficiency of data transmission significantly.

The new systems offer a much better deal for the user, irrespective as to who may provide the service. The optical fibres that will be installed are easier and more efficient to use than metal wires and the signal is stronger, cutting down the number of boosting stations needed along the line. Lower costs, better signal quality, the ability to send voice or data over the same lines and faster transmission speeds are all promised over the next five years, the period needed to replace existing equipment.

The effect of satellites

The one area the PTTs will not give up without a fight is the control of the radio wavelengths now that satellites are becoming a standard part of the communications mix and are becoming easier to put in orbit through the space shuttle program and Europe's limited ability to put its own rockets into space. Satellite communication removes the need for land lines and the capacity of a modern satellite to transmit messages is very large.

Satellites open up the way for international video-conferencing, whereby groups of people can talk to and look at other groups over long distances. Video-conferencing has not caught on in the UK in spite of the availability of conferencing facilities from British Telecom. More importantly, commercial satellites will get around the ability of PTTs to limit access to existing satellite capacity and this will be a way for Mercury to build up an international network.

IBM's joint venture in this area may be just as significant as AT & T's move into computers. IBM has joined with Comstat, which specialises in satellite technology, and Aetna, a large insurance company, to form Satellite Business Systems to provide the total communications needs of large companies. Messages that are bounced up to the satellite and back again are automatically distributed by the network at speeds comparable to those used by computers internally. Communication at this speed between one SBS subscriber and another makes feasible the quick and cost effective movement of large amounts of data between one enterprise and another. Add to this IBM's increasing interest in PABX through another joint venture and the prospect opens up for a separate communications network for large corporations to be established over the next few years.

Communicating with a centralised data base

Many companies have the need to connect remote sites to a centralised data base. Where the need is significant then the company will set up its own communication system. A good example is a US-based finance company, ACC, which has over 60 branches throughout the UK. Each office is connected to a central computer in the US which manages all the paperwork, including credit checking and accounts. Offices can be kept to an easily manageable size, with staff concentrating on their prime function of selling the company's financial services.

Time-sharing bureaux

Where it is not possible to justify dedicated computer facilities, companies use a time-sharing bureau. These bureaux connect subscribers to a suite of powerful central computers that hold individual programs for each set of subscribers. The best known network is that run by General Electric in the US through its subsidiary, GEISCO. A call to a local number enables a terminal to be connected through a modem to GEISCO's system, which includes 450 computers which connect more than 26 countries. Over 6,000 users can access the network at the same time and the application of message switching technology is such that large users can be given the impression that the whole network has been dedicated to them on a continuous basis. Thus a multinational company can use GEISCO to consolidate its international accounts, with each separate company submitting its financial information to the central computer, which can then transform the data into higher level consolidations.

Video-based information systems

Video-based information systems can use television channels to broadcast news pages called up through the telephone network to join subscribers to the central data base. The use of television channels for services such as Ceefax and Oracle in the UK and Keyfax in the US, is known as teletext; this is relatively inexpensive as it uses the intervals in the transmission of television pictures to send out its pages of text and graphics. The information is continuously transmitted to the subscriber, who uses a special decoder to display the pages. The capacity of teletext is limited because of this continuous transmission and by the amount of information that can be shown on each page. It is therefore only used for information that has general appeal and needs constant updating, such as the news or the weather forecast.

The telephone network carries two types of video-based systems, videotex and on-line data bases.

Videotex systems

Videotex systems include Prestel in the UK, Telidon in Canada and Minitel in France; AT & T, among others, is developing a system in the US. Videotex is a two-way system where the receiver controls what information he should be sent. Videotex can either select data from a range of information providers, for news, stock market prices or whatever, or be interactive with electronic mail or home shopping facilities. Its two-way nature has been used by travel agents in the UK, who make up over 20 per cent of Prestel's subscribers, to check on flight schedules or to book airline reservations by connections through Prestel to the airline's computer.

Prestel's graphics quality is disappointing, but this is due mainly to a trade-off between speed and quality. A page of Prestel graphics is filled in about ten seconds, while Telidon's far more attractive pictures take three times as long to transmit and require more expensive equipment. Videotex signals are sent out by the subscriber on quite slow channels, as requests are made on a keyboard and take time to be completed. Responses are sent back at about 1,200 bits per second, which is about as much as the telephone lines can carry.

The growth of videotex has been slow, due mostly to the reluctance of the subscriber to pay for the information he is able to receive. Prestel goes out mainly to commercial customers, such as travel agents, and with only 30,000 subscribers can hardly be termed a success. Minitel may see the first major application of this technology, as the French Government is planning to distribute over 300,000 free to its telephone subscribers, initially as a replacement for telephone directories.

Videotex was designed at a time when personal computers were not available and was intended to bring the power of a central computer to subscribers who could not afford to maintain a large data base. Its development has undoubtedly been slowed down by the introduction of microcomputers, but will probably increase as the same computers can be used as intelligent terminals, interfacing with public or private data bases on principles similar to time-sharing on mainframe computers. An interesting development has been the introduction of Micronet, which delivers software programs over Prestel directly to the subscriber's home computer, removing the need to copy out programs from magazines: this could make Prestel more attractive to non-business users, as there are now some 1 million home computers in the UK alone.

On-line financial information services

Accessing on-line data bases is of great importance to the financial community, who need prompt delivery of news, rates and prices to function effectively. Prestel has set up its own services, such as Fintel in conjunction with. the *Financial Times*, to provide information on financial markets.

While several companies use Prestel to set up private videotex systems, others provide the same facilities from their own computer network. In the UK, The Stock Exchange has introduced its own service, Topic, to compete directly with the earlier established Datastream. Both provide information on companies quoted on the UK stock exchanges, as well as price information which is kept up-to-date while the markets are open. Information from other markets, such as the financial futures or the commodities markets, is also provided. Topic is a separate computer system which provides the videotex services generated from another computer that holds the data base and updates the data as the need arises.

The best known of these financial information services is Reuters. Reuters began in the nineteenth century as a fast news service for the financial markets, using a network of correspondents to cable news of share prices from the Continent to London. Coverage of general news was added later and the concept of a press agency was born. The capability of the Reuters network was such that no single newspaper could match it and in 1925 the Press Association, owned by UK provincial newspapers, acquired it. After the Second World War ownership was extended to include first the National Press Association, owned by the big Fleet Street newspapers, and later the press associations in Australia and New Zealand.

Reuters did not fare well with its news services and returned to its original business, financial information. It developed a system to complement its tele-type services, which enabled brokers to get share prices on a video screen by using a special terminal. In 1971 Reuters started to extend these services to the foreign exchange and money markets and after initial resistance became essential to the operation of dealing rooms at a time when rate volatility increased sharply following the first oil price shock. The number of subscribers rose from five in 1973 to over 30,000 in 1982, with installations in over 100 countries.

This initial success was masked by the need to invest substantially in new equipment, totalling more than £80 million. Services to other financial users, such as shipbrokers, were added and over 45 separate financial information services are now available. A new service, which enables foreign exchange dealers to contact each other directly through the Reuters terminal, cost more than £8 million to develop. The direct dealer service enables dealers in one bank to communicate with dealers in another bank anywhere in the world: contracts are discussed in a conversational manner and entered into on a secure basis, with hard copy of the conversation printed out on the Reuters teletype. The investment is on such a scale as to make entry to this market dauntingly expensive and Reuters has only one serious rival, Telerate, a US-based service that is starting to expand aggressively overseas.

Reuters and its competitors have networks of computers which are linked to switching gear, which for a large user is often on the subscriber's premises, permitting the subscriber access to those services he is paying for. The infor-mation is supplied by market makers, who rent space to display their prices and can control access to those pages. The quality of the information is not a function of the computerised system, but is only as good as the person putting it in.

When we look at how the foreign exchange and money markets work we will see how to use specific information provided on a typical Reuters page. The most impressive of Reuters' present services is the Dealing Service. This uses an advanced terminal, managed by a microprocessor, which has several special features in addition to the normal typewriter style keyboard. The main use of the special keys is to connect the dealer to other banks by using a four-character code; connection time averages four seconds, irrespective of the location of the bank being called, which could be in a different country or continent. Once connected, information is requested through the keyboard, which can store precoded messages to speed up communication. Thus the message 'please advise your spot rates' is passed by using a very short abbreviation, CCYSP, which puts the full message in front of the receiver. The asker will also precode his order 'OK I buy $1,000,000 at' to get the price he has seen by using his short code message and the two numbers needed to signify the rate. The person making the quotation can always interrupt the person asking for rates to change a quotation already given, although with the short codes, he has to be pretty quick; in the event of a tie, when a rate giver tries to change the rate while the receiver is simultaneously trying to deal at that rate, the rate giver will always win. This type of communication reproduces the way deals are made over the telephone or telex.

Conversations are shown on a screen that is divided into five areas, including one area showing the status of the system at the present time. A second area holds a news service which gives the dealer headlines concerning important financial news that may concern him – he can see the news without having to stop whatever else he is doing. A third area is large enough to hold the full information given on a standard rate screen. This area can also be used for conversation by removing the rate information from the screen. The main conversational window is on the bottom portion of the screen. Two conversations can be held at the same time and it is possible to switch easily between the two. Access to the system is password-controlled and all conversations are printed out on paper showing the time the conversation took place and which terminals were involved. The fifth element of the screen shows the calls being made or the short code of the banks which are trying to contact the dealer; the receiving dealer can select the order in which he responds to these calls. The dealer calling in can leave a message on this part of the screen if he cannot get through immediately. The Dealing Service is an outstanding example of modern communications technology.

British Telecom itself is also introducing new services. One of these, the City Business System, is aimed directly at the financial market. CBS is a computer-based telephone system that replaces with a video screen all the telephone lines coming into the desk of a dealer or trader. A busy dealer or broker could have well over 50 telephone lines competing for his attention. Once the protective covers are lifted away the inside of his desk resembles a plate of extremely fine, interwoven spaghetti. A large number of these wires connect the dealer to a counterparty directly, bypassing the switchboard, and terminating in a press button on the dealer's board that lights up each time either party activates the line. Each wire has to be individually matched up between the telephone line and the light on the board that carries the name of the party concerned. Moving a dealer from one part of the room to another can be a nightmare.

CBS has at its heart a computer that can be connected to over 1,000 telephone lines and can serve over 500 dealer stations. The computer is activated by means of a screen. Infra-red beams create an invisible grid over the face of the screen and if the grid is broken by a finger or a pencil the co-ordinate sends signals to the computer. Telephone lines are shown as boxes holding the name of the other party. A touch on the screen is all that is needed to dial automatically numbers that are frequently required or to connect with a direct line. A number that has not been stored in the system is dialled by touching a dial pad in the corner of the screen. Incoming calls are shown on the screen as a flashing box, so that the dealer can see who is calling and if necessary he can decide the order in which he answers. The computer holds up to 5,000 pages of data and can access the data bases of other computers. The screens can be individually structured by the dealer to show telephone lines and data. Incoming calls can always be seen on the bottom of the screen.

There is no longer any need to rewire desks, as every dealer station can be programmed individually to access any of the 1,000 lines that the computer can manage. By use of a small keyboard, text can be entered in the system and then sent as a message by telex or lodged in the data base of a computer. Later developments will enable subscribers to use and read Prestel through the VDU. CBS is not cheap to install, but it is certainly at the forefront of modern technology.

It was the successful Wall Street launch of Telerate, valuing the company at around US $900 million, that caused the City to view Reuters in a new light, particularly as the largest shareholders, Exco, are a leading firm of money brokers in London. Telerate's success stems from 1978, when the New York foreign exchange markets opened up. Telerate appeared in London shortly afterwards and is now expanding rapidly around the world, as it finds its international business more profitable than its US-based activities. Telerate markets its products outside North America through a joint venture with the Associated Press and Dow Jones and the Dow Jones news of US financial markets is a strong feature of the package, as is its relative cheapness compared with Reuters. Telerate offers some 10,000 pages of information, but presents them as information pages, rather than showing pages in the raw form sent in by subscribers.

Telerate is following the same course as Reuters and is developing an intelligent terminal, an IBM-compatible microcomputer, which will be designed to speed up the time it takes to retrieve the pages that the subscriber needs most often. The next stage would seem to be to provide software that enables the user to use the data on those pages to generate information to meet his individual requirements.

Neither Reuters nor Telerate provides a particularly cheap service to their subscribers. Their success shows the commercial value of being able to communicate information quickly to people who need to see it. The convergence of the communication and computer industries will mean major changes in the way that offices work and are organised. These changes will need considerable investment and implementation may require considerable management effort if the best results are to be obtained.

CHAPTER 6

Changing office systems

The first appearances of video screens in offices followed the computerisation of one of the basic office tools, the typewriter. As companies grow there is a continual conflict between the need to keep everyone informed, usually with the generation of bureaucratic instructions, and the need to reduce flows of paper to cut costs and let people get on with their work. Modern office machinery is definitely on the side of the paper generators. The first developments were the fast photocopier, designed by Xerox, and typewriters with memories, enabling word processing to be performed. Word processing enables text to be edited with the minimum of effort.

Word processors

The intelligent typewriter is the first element of the office of the future. The first word processors had magnetic cards to store text and found their application in lawyers' or company secretaries' offices, where long, complex text is used frequently with only a few changes needed to adapt the document from one purpose to another. Memory storage in the typewriter was only sufficient to hold a few lines, which could be inspected as the typist entered the text and changed if necessary. Word processors have evolved into full computer systems, dedicated to the preparation of text; until the adaptation of the new generation of integrated software to word processors, these systems will only handle text and cannot be used for graphics or calculations.

A modern word processor creates a document without paper and stores it to disc; the document is read on a screen and can be amended at any time. When the document is in a satisfactory state it is then usually printed out and duplicates photocopied. Distribution is by mail or by facsimile transmission, which is the sending of documents through a scanner linked to the telephone network: a 'faxed' page of a document takes about one minute to transmit.

Teletex

A faster means of document transmission will be provided by teletex, not to be confused with videotex. A teletex machine stores the message in memory before transmitting it over a telephone line to the memory of the receiving teletex terminal; the speed of transmission is some 45 times faster than telex and documents can be presented in much better fashion. Teletex will be introduced throughout Europe over the next few years. One advantage will be that word processors will be able to transmit messages to teletex terminals, in the same way that they now can send them over the telex network, without any paper needing to be produced.

Microfiche

Filing and storing the great quantities of paper generated in a modern office is a major headache. Documents can be filed in paper form or on microfiche (on a word processor the original also remains on the original disc until it is erased). Microfiche holds the document in the form of miniature photographic images that can be enlarged and read on a small projector and is a convenient way to hold large quantities of information. In a bank, for example, it is used to store media such as physical copies of cancelled cheques or customer instructions. Indexing is of great importance for swift retrieval of documents.

Electronic mail

The next stage in office automation is well developed, the use of electronic mail. Users have their own terminals which are linked to central computers, usually in a bureau operated by an independent company, although larger corporations use their own facilities. Messages are sent electronically and read on the terminal by one or more recipients. The system files the messages in special or general files held for the individual user and material can be deleted at any time to keep the files tidy. Electronic mail is intended to reduce paper flow and improve secretarial productivity by enabling formal or informal messages to be sent quickly and effectively. Once the text handling facilities are improved, the terminals will be used for a far greater variety of work. Electronic mail is password-controlled and has a fairly high level of security. Its use is spreading rapidly and will accelerate with the introduction of common standards of transmission on an international scale.

Through the packet switching network operated by British Telecom, electronic mail can be sent between different companies, the first step towards a truly paperless society. Portable terminals extend the reach of the system even further.

Computer networks

The greatest efficiencies that will follow from all of these terminals sprouting up around the office will come from the introduction of networks that enable telex machines, word processors and central data bases to converse easily with each other. Xerox's Ethernet is being accepted as a standard that will enable different types of terminals to talk to each other and other suppliers, such as Wang, offer alternatives. There are two approaches. One is to have all the terminals feed into a central computer, usually a minicomputer, which redistributes documents or provides users with a centralised data base. This can be used for linking a secretary's word processor to the boss's terminal so that he can inspect and if necessary amend any typing before it goes out. Many large companies use what are in effect non-interactive, that is, dumb, terminals to extract information on performance, industrial statistics or personnel. The second approach is to use a local area network, such as Ethernet, to connect microcomputers, including word processors, together.

All of these developments are predicated by the achievement of machine-to-machine communication, a topic that is much discussed and for which several products are theoretically available, although the performance and capability of these products tend to fall short of the claims made for them.

In the office itself the main developments concern local area networks, such as Ethernet discussed above. Local area networks come in several configurations. They can be arranged in rings, where the various peripherals are connected to a continuous circuit; a problem is the need to boost the signal as it travels around the ring. Ethernet uses a broadcast network, with each terminal connected by a transmitter/receiver – a transceiver – to the coaxial cable which links all the equipment together. Each terminal takes from the network messages that have been addressed to it by reading the coded address of each message as it goes past.

A third approach is similar to a telephone exchange and has all the peripherals coming into a central switching centre; this is generally referred to as a star system and is the usual way mainframe-based data processing networks are set up.

Telephone companies foresee that the office of the future will be centred around the telephone network, which will be run by a major computer system. This computer will form the PABX and will sit in the middle of every conversation and distribute data and telephone calls around the network. All parts of the enterprise can be linked to the PABX which will handle all written and spoken communications. Computers, typewriters, copying and filing machines, telephones, cellular radio, video and printing devices will all be linked through the computer at the heart of the PABX through a broadwaveband cable network. Digital-based communications are essential for this to work. We will have to wait to see if this materialises, but the increased competition that comes from deregulation brings the possibility much closer.

A major problem is that to send different types of information – voice, video or data – requires different communications bandwidths, and the wider the bandwidth the higher the cost.

The electronic office of the future

When the electronic office is perfected, all its occupants will be connected to a network through computers similar to the Apple Lisa. All internal communications and most external communications will be sent by and read on these intelligent terminals and filing will be held centrally for common documents or privately for sensitive material. Computers will be connected to machines resembling photocopiers or to laser printers, capable of producing colour documents as well as text, and used for producing high-class output to be sent to the company's customers. All managers will have small, paperback-sized computers which will have sufficient capacity to hold several days' work and will be capable of connection to the network at any time through the telephone. Small, portable computers that fit easily into a briefcase are already available. For example, Tandy's Model 100 comes with built-in software for record keeping, a diary and rudimentary word processing, as well as a built-in modem that enables the computer to act as a terminal or for electronic mail.

When he gets home the manager will use his television set as the screen for his computer. Home television will be in modular form, with a high resolution screen acting as the output for several services, such as television stations, video recorders, computers and interactive videotex, connecting the house to shops, banks and information services. Television sets are now available that have 'windows' on the main screen enabling the viewer to watch two channels at the same time. Thus the manager could be working with his computer system while calling up an external data base or keeping track of a football game while wrestling with his household accounts. In all probability, the manager will only rarely have to go into his office, as all the material he needs to work with can be supplied electronically to his computer. Office work will be mainly taken up with meetings with colleagues or with customers.

The rapid pace of change is made more difficult to assimilate as microprocessors find their ways into all types of office equipment. Word processors will get additional features, dumb terminals will develop new skills and the humble telephone switchboard will become a sophisticated piece of equipment. Buying these systems becomes difficult, as the threat of obsolescence of new equipment before it can pay for itself is once again a major problem. In addition, prices will fall, but the timing of that fall will be difficult to predict; there is nothing worse than buying equipment that falls dramatically in price shortly after the purchase has been completed.

Corporations will have to re-organise their data processing and office management departments into information technology management groups to control the rapid growth of new electronic equipment throughout the company. The personal computer has brought increases in clerical productivity to the management process and this will accelerate as the ability to get into the company's main data base improves. At some stage it will be better to stop buying small systems in a piecemeal fashion and to go back to centralised control of systems development. At present, however, most companies seem happy to let the use of small computers proliferate to see how their use will grow before bringing the activities together again under a formalised framework.

Each of the technological developments we have been considering, covering computers and telecommunications, has special significance for the participants in the financial markets, where information is at a premium. The growth of the financial markets means increasing demands for faster communications and greater processing capacity. Success in these markets now depends on using the tools of the modern office in the most effective way.

Part Two

The business of money

CHAPTER 7

Introduction to the money markets

We all know about money, it touches every aspect of our lives, our work and our leisure. The supply of money is a prime concern for the individuals who earn or own it and for the governments which control it. The balance is precarious: too little and living standards fall, too much and inflation takes hold. Users of money borrow or lend funds in their local money markets; for them the critical factor is the future behaviour of interest rates. To anticipate possible changes in interest rates requires an understanding of the structure of the market and of the players in it.

The gold standard

The history of foreign exchange is one of an international financial system looking for ways equitably to express the value of one currency for another. Up to the First World War this was achieved by the gold standard, originally based on the physical movement of gold, later evolving into paper money backed by holdings of the metal in central banks. Exchange rates were stable, which was important in times of slow communications, and fixed to the value of gold.

However, during the First World War governments printed far more money than their holdings of gold could cover, leading to the suspension of the gold standard. Its re-introduction after the war was not successful, as the economic consequences of the war led to increasing domestic instability within most countries, with constant devaluations against gold and the introduction of exchange controls. By 1931 the UK had given up the gold standard and by 1936 the use of the gold standard had effectively ended throughout the world.

In 1935 the US adopted the modified gold standard; within this international convention governments would sell gold only to other governments, the free movement of gold was prohibited and the price of gold was fixed at US $35 per oz, a price that remained unchanged until 1971. The Second World War led to the suspension of this arrangement. The Bretton Woods conference of 1944 ratified this into the gold exchange standard and agreed to the formation of the International Monetary Fund (IMF) to regulate the international market. Member countries agreed to keep their currencies fixed to gold or the US dollar, which effectively became a reserve currency and thus the predominant means for central banks to intervene in the world markets; the US dollar replaced sterling as the most common currency used for international trade.

Eurocurrency markets

By 1952 the international markets were re-opening, dealing departments were re-established in London banks and authorised banks around Europe began dealing in spot and forward transactions. A pool of homeless international funds, the Eurodollar market, started to develop in the late 1950s. Introduction of exchange controls in the UK in 1957 and of interest equalisation tax in the US in 1963, together with the deficits in the US economy throughout the 1960s, helped that development considerably, centred originally in London, but now spread throughout the world. Eurocurrencies are unregulated and rates are very competitive; where exchange controls do not exist, domestic rates tend to determine the Eurorates, although domestic regulation and reserve requirements must be taken account when comparing the two. While the Eurocurrency markets may to some extent offset the effectiveness of central banks in controlling domestic affairs, they represent an important source of liquidity for governments and corporations and provide a backcloth to the foreign exchange markets.

Smithsonian Agreement

During the 1950s and 1960s there were continuing adjustments to the mechanics of the gold exchange system, with constant devaluations, revaluations and pressure on particular currencies, notably sterling, and in 1967 a run on gold itself. The stability of the dollar, however, kept the system intact until 1970, when US gold reserves had fallen to US $11 billion, while overseas claims amounted to US $22 billion. The US had massive budget deficits which, together with a lack of internal controls and low domestic interest rates, led to massive outflows of capital from the US to Europe, increasing the value of the European currencies against the dollar.

In August 1971, after the markets had been closed for several days, the US abandoned dollar–gold convertibility and most currencies were allowed to float. The resulting instability led to the 'Group of Ten' countries formulating the Smithsonian Agreement: the gold price was raised to US $38 per oz; individual countries revalued their currencies against the dollar; non-dollar currencies were to be allowed to fluctuate against each other by plus or minus 4.5 per cent. After a temporary lull, speculative movements of capital led to the effective collapse of the Smithsonian Agreement by 1973. The value of free gold rose sharply and by 1975 the official gold price was abolished, with central banks buying and selling without restriction in the free gold market. The floating rate system has survived major crises of economic instability and massive inflation caused by increases in oil prices. It is unlikely that the floating rate system will change in the near future.

The European Monetary System and the ECU

A good example of controlled floating is the European Monetary System. The EMS is an attempt to create a zone of relatively stable exchange rates between member countries of the EEC and to replace the European currency 'snake' first introduced in 1971. Established in 1979 the EMS exchange rate arrangements cover all EEC members, other than Greece and the UK.

The European Currency Unit (ECU), which is the unit of account used by EEC central banks, is derived from a basket of nine European currencies. Within the EMS each member country establishes a central rate for its currencies against the ECU; thus a grid of cross rates can be drawn up against the other ECU currencies. No currency can deviate by more than plus or minus 2.25 per cent from the middle rate established for these cross rates, with the exception of the lira which can deviate by plus or minus 6 per cent.

Limits are also set for each currency against its ECU central rate. These limits are set more tightly than those for the cross rates to ensure that action is taken before possible harm is done to another currency in the EMS. This limit is set at 0.75 of the margin allowed for cross rates (that is, $2.25 \times 0.75 = 1.7$ per cent for most currencies), with provision for some adjustments relating to the size of the economy and the heavy bias that may be caused by extraordinary movement in sterling or lira. Once a currency has deviated to a point where it is breaking one or other of its limits then the central bank must correct the situation through internal action (for example, raising the discount rate), revaluation, intervention in the foreign exchange market or other economic policy measures.

The ECU is constructed from its nine constituent currencies. To express an ECU in terms of the Deutschmark the individual weighting of each currency is multiplied by its exchange rate against the Deutschmark (see Table 7.1).

Table 7.1　An ECU expressed in terms of Deutschmarks

	Amount of currency in ECU		Deutschmark exchange rate		Currency amount of Deutschmarks in ECU
Deutschmark	0.71900	×	1.0000	=	0.7190
French franc	1.31000	÷	3.0640	=	0.4275
Pound sterling	0.08780	×	3.7315	=	0.3276
Guilder	0.25600	÷	1.1275	=	0.2271
Belgian franc	3.71000	÷	20.2000	=	0.1837
Lira	140.00000	÷	616.5000	=	0.2271
Danish krone	0.21900	÷	3.6061	=	0.0607
Punt	0.00871	×	3.0969	=	0.0270
Drachma	1.15000	÷	40.7450	=	0.0282
Luxembourg franc	0.14000	÷	20.2000	=	0.0069
					2.2348

Special Drawing Rights

The IMF has its own composite currency, the Special Drawing Right, or SDR, which is used by members of the IMF as a reserve asset to supplement their usual gold and currency reserves. Originally linked to gold, SDRs were introduced by the IMF in 1968. In 1974 the SDR's link to gold was cut and since that time it has been constructed by reference to a basket made up of the major trading currencies. From 1974 to 1980 this basket comprised 16 currencies, with an amendment to the composition and weighting of the basket in 1978. The IMF had been seeking ways to increase the use and acceptability of the SDR and to achieve this it simplified the SDR to the five-currency basket, introduced on 1 January 1981. This latest change has not significantly changed the value of the SDR, but has made it considerably easier to calculate exchange and deposit rates for SDR-denominated instruments.

The composition of the SDR as redefined on 1 January 1981 is shown in Table 7.2.

Table 7.2   Composition of the SDR on 1 January 1981

	Weight (%)	Amount of currency in one SDR
US dollar	42	0.540
Deutschmark	19	0.460
Japanese yen	13	34.000
French franc	13	0.740
Pound sterling	13	0.071
	100	

The IMF publishes daily an SDR exchange rate (the 'IMF rate') based on the mid spot rates provided at noon each day by the Bank of England for each of the constituent currencies. This SDR exchange rate is officially announced at midday in Washington, DC (about 4 p.m. GMT). In London the *Financial Times* issues a daily breakdown of exchange rates for various currencies against the SDR.

The composite currencies are relatively more stable in exchange rate terms than the individual currencies that go into the baskets, while the interest rates available for investments denominated in the composite currencies are attractive, even compared with the individual currencies themselves. The currency hedge implicit in the structure of the SDR and the ECU adds to their attraction as investment media.

Domestic money markets

The foreign exchange markets originate in the domestic money markets for the currencies involved. The availability of those currencies is controlled by the central banks which manage them. The power of a central bank reflects its importance in the control of the supply of money, physically through the printing press or through regulation of the banking system. All money flows through the banking system. A loan made to one person is used to buy goods or services and the proceeds from the sale are deposited in another bank. Slowing down the speed at which money goes around is a factor in controlling money supply and ensuring that not all money deposited can be re-lent helps ensure prudence with regard to the financial strength of the banking community.

Money markets, where local currency is traded, usually grew up around the needs of the government to raise funds to balance spending, supplement taxes or pay for wars. Money markets are supervised by central banks, which intervene in the markets to control the supply of money or to raise funds for the government. Each country has developed in different ways and the depth of local money markets has been caused by a mixture of historical and organisational factors.

To understand how to use money we first need to look at the money markets themselves. In this part of the book we will look more closely at the problems of market users (investors as well as borrowers), for example, a treasurer of a trading company looking for working capital. In addition to borrowers and lenders, the users of the market, there are a large number of traders buying and selling instruments for gain, holding positions against movements in interest rates or other factors that affect the underlying value of the paper, such as the changes in the balance of payments that could affect the value of government securities. The traders' activities are both more specialised and more complex than the market users', but the principles underlying their trading are much the same. We will look at them from the viewpoint of a direct participant in the market and then will look at how a bank manages its treasury operations.

CHAPTER 8

The UK and US money markets and banking systems

To understand the complex forms that money takes we shall now look at the UK and US money markets in some detail. These markets are free of exchange controls, which apply in varying degrees to most other money markets in the world. Exchange controls limit the movement of funds and create imperfections that will affect the behaviour of the currency being controlled. Neither the UK nor the US can be taken as the model for any other money market, but both are well developed and the US market, which has grown up around a much more constrained banking sector, is quite different from those found in Europe. We will start with the London markets.

UK MARKETS

Role of the Bank of England

Central banking was first successfully practised by the Bank of England (founded in 1694 to manage the national debt and until nationalisation in 1946 an independent bank in its own right). Operating under the direction of the Treasury, the Bank has a monopoly for printing bank notes and minting coins in the UK, implements fiscal policy and acts as lender of last resort to the money market, thus influencing directly the level of interest rates in that market.

The Bank of England controls the City of London through a series of private 'clubs', using the network of discount houses, acceptance houses, clearing banks and brokers to keep the system tidy. Reliance on keeping order through persuasion rather than by legal regulation has created a unique business climate which enables London to continue to develop its position as the leading financial centre in the world.

Money supply

Governments create money through financing fiscal deficits, buying bonds from the public and by intervention in the foreign exchange market. Secondary monetary expansion comes through the commercial banks as a consequence of government activity. The bank multiplier, given a demand for funds, is a function of the amount of reserves or reserve assets held at the direction of the central bank. A 10 per cent reserve gives a multiplier of 9:1, a 5 per cent reserve 19:1. While money supply may be an important determinant in the growth of nominal gross domestic product (GDP), the effect of an increase in money supply will depend on the amount of spare capacity in the economy and, if the economy is dependent on international trade, on movements in the exchange rate. With excess capacity, an increase in money supply will raise economic activity or increase inflation. Money supply growth is therefore a preoccupation of the central bank and its efforts to control it will have an impact on interest rates, which are often used directly in this effort.

Types of money markets

London has several financial markets: the insurance market, The Stock Exchange, the commodities markets, the financial futures markets, the money markets, and the foreign exchange market. To some degree these overlap. The sterling money market is based on the dealings between the discount market and what are known as the parallel money markets, notably the interbank market, local authorities market, sterling certificate of deposit market, finance house market and the more or less dormant intercompany market. The sterling money market exists side by side with the Eurocurrency markets, including the market for Eurosterling.

The discount market is made up of 11 members of the London Discount Market Association, two discount brokers and the money traders of the large commercial banks. Lending is predominantly secured, with the Bank of England acting as lender of last resort, thus ensuring the prime aim of the market, the provision of a safe, but profitable, source of liquidity. The main functions of the discount houses are to make markets for call money, Treasury bills, commercial bills and other short-term instruments.

As the name implies, call money is placed with a financial institution without a fixed maturity date and can be withdrawn at any time with a telephone call. Banks place large amounts of money at call with discount houses, receiving in return a rate very close to the yield obtained by the discount houses from investments made in a variety of instruments, mainly commercial and Treasury bills.

Treasury bills are short-term instruments issued by the government; the undoubted quality of the issuer and their short-term maturity make Treasury bills the most marketable of all money market instruments. In the UK, Treasury bills are bearer documents issued weekly by the Bank of England, usually for 91 days, and underwritten by the discount houses.

Commercial bills are 'two name' paper, with the names of the drawer and the acceptor on them. Usually self-liquidating trade finance, they resemble post-dated cheques and can be sold for cash at a discount. Commercial bills, or bankers' acceptances, provide relatively low interest rate credit to a borrower and a marketable security to the bank. They are created by the bank's customer drawing a bill or draft on the bank, which then accepts the bill by adding its name to the paper. By this acceptance, the bank promises to pay the face value of the bill to its holders. The resulting paper is extremely marketable, assuming that the bank has a firm position in the market, shown, for example, by its status with the Bank of England.

The Bank of England now controls the liquidity in the money market by open market operations in the commercial bill market, rather than by lending at the discount window in its role as lender of last resort. This enables market forces to have greater influence in the setting of interest rate levels. This was part of a wide range of new measures introduced in 1980 and 1981 which included the classification of banks into authorised banks, whose size and standing must meet certain criteria, and licensed deposit takers, who must use this description in their titles to show that those criteria have not been met. In addition, the Bank of England differentiates between banks whose acceptances are eligible for rediscount with the Bank of England and those whose acceptances are ineligible.

Eligible banks may accept commercial bills that meet the Bank of England's requirements for eligibility, normally the financing of trade for not more than 187 days. Discount houses will invest in these acceptances, which provide liquid assets should the commercial banks suddenly withdraw call money, as the eligible bills in their portfolios can always be sold to the Bank of England to replace the loss of liquidity. To ensure that the discount houses have the funds they need to build up their portfolios all eligible banks have to keep 4 per cent of their eligible liabilities with the discount houses in cash, earning a rate of interest somewhat below market rates.

The largest of the parallel markets is the interbank market. Dealings are between banks, generally for short-term transactions that are unsecured and are not negotiable or transferable. As seen above, liquidity is provided by the discount market. The banks use the market to manage the differences between their assets and liabilities and to determine the pricing for loans and deposits through the London Interbank Offered Rate, or LIBOR. The market is well served by brokers, who provide the means of putting buyers together with sellers quickly and efficiently. Brokers act in all the London financial markets and their independence is promoted and protected by the Bank of England. The interbank market is well developed, with most transactions taking place with same-day value.

Industrial companies and non-banking financial institutions borrow money from or deposit funds with the money markets, usually in the banking system, or through the purchase of securities from the stock market or the discount houses.

Banking

The main activity of commercial banks is interest differential business, the lending of funds at, hopefully, hgher rates than those paid for deposits. This lending is financed by a bank's capital, its retail deposits and funds raised in the money markets. An alternative source of finance, usually used by smaller companies or individuals, are the finance houses, who make up an important subsection of the market. Merchant banks tend to concentrate on fee-earning and trade-related business, leaving day-to-day banking to be provided by the commercial banks; one of their important functions is the raising of long-term or permanent funds from the stock market.

Over 650 banking institutions now contribute to the statistics used to determine the monetary sector. These can be divided into the London clearing banks, Scottish and Northern Ireland clearing banks, accepting houses, overseas banks, consortium banks, licensed deposit takers, discount houses, Trustees Savings Banks and the National Girobank. Banking in the UK has seen considerable growth. For instance, the overseas banks, mostly in London to take part in the Eurocurrency markets, grew in number from 163 in 1970 to 353 in 1980.

Basic services

Bank products have not changed much in the last few years, although many money markets do not offer the range of services available in the UK. The basic product is a current account, where traditionally deposits do not earn interest and are withdrawn by means of cheques or transfers on demand by the customer, without notice, but within the physical constraints of the banking system. Where agreed the customer may borrow money by overdrawing the account: the bank may demand repayment at any time. Interest is payable on the daily outstanding overdraft and normally charged at a margin (or spread) over the bank's base rate for the currency. The base rate is a practical way to apply an easily varied interest rate to a multitude of often small, fluctuating accounts. Penal rates are applied if the customer exceeds his agreed credit line or where no credit line exists.

Current accounts provide a convenient way to handle unreliable timing of cash flows – the unreliability was generally due in the past to the time needed to move paper from one location to another.

Other products include loans and deposits, of both fixed and non-fixed maturities and trade financing through bills, letters of credit and foreign exchange. Bank loans and other financings are relatively straightforward to understand. Investing funds is, however, a much more confusing process, with a wide range of instruments offered by banks, building societies, fund managers, savings institutions and the government.

Certificates of deposit

Over 100 banks issue primary sterling certificates of deposit (CDs), which are unsecured paper, ineligible as security or for rediscount at the Bank of England. A CD is a confirmation that a sum of money has been deposited with a bank at an agreed rate for an agreed time. The confirmation is negotiable and banks and discount houses create a secondary market where CDs can be bought or sold prior to maturity. Investors will, depending on the credit standing of the issuing bank, usually accept a lower rate of interest on a CD than on the most usual alternative, a time deposit (which is an amount of money placed for a fixed time at a fixed interest rate), as the CD can be liquidated at any time without asking the bank to break the deposit (which for a time deposit could result in paying a penalty, particularly if rates have gone up since the deposit was originally placed). CDs are mainly held by banks and discount houses as liquid investments.

Local authority bonds

Local authorities issue bills for periods of up to 12 months and bonds for up to five years. Bills are generally rediscountable at the Bank of England and regulations exist linking the size and tenor of issue to the income from rates an individual authority enjoys. Local authority bonds, while not rediscountable with the Bank of England, are easily transferable.

Liquidity ratios

Each deposit taker now has a liquidity ratio, individually agreed with the Bank of England, based on its liquidity needs for the future and designed to ensure that the institution can meet any demand for withdrawals. In addition, the Bank of England monitors foreign currency exposure, including country and sovereign risk, of banks with international operations.

Guidelines covering day-to-day exposure are that no bank will exceed 15 per cent of its capital base for the aggregate net short open position in all currencies, including sterling, and will not exceed 10 per cent in any one currency.

Retail banking

Retail banking is carried out through the branch networks of the clearing banks, with increasing competition for deposits coming from institutions such as the building societies and government-owned activities such as the National Girobank and the Trustees Savings Banks. The clearers offer similar rates for savings and deposit accounts; these were historically fixed by a cartel arrangement disbanded by the introduction of competition and credit control in 1971, although competition has done little to differentiate the pricing of products and services.

Retail banking is outside the general scope of most financial managers, but the changes in retail banking may have an impact on the wholesale markets that we are looking at. These include the increasing competition between the clearers and the building society movement, diversification of the money brokers and discount houses into 'bank-like' activities, and the greater awareness of consumers of recently introduced products such as money market accounts or alternatives such as offshore currency funds.

US MARKETS

The City can be likened to an onion – you have to peel away the protective layers to get to the Bank of England sitting snugly at the centre. Its structure is quite unusual. While the money markets in the US developed in a completely different way, they are more representative of financial centres around the world. However, the range of instruments traded is far more extensive than in most other markets.

Banking

After the War of Independence, New York soon took over as the main banking centre in the US. By 1825 the three present-day leading banks in the US, Bank of America, Citibank and Chase Manhattan had all been founded in New York (Bank of America was later to migrate to the West Coast).

Banking in the US is run on quite different terms compared with the UK and is far more constrained by legal and regulatory systems. Banks are looked on with some suspicion and the blame for the Great Crash of 1929 and the Great Depression that followed still rests firmly and with some justification on the banking system.

Federal Reserve System

Overseeing the banking system in the US is the Federal Reserve System (the 'Fed'), comprising a board of governors, the Federal Open Market Committee, 12 federal reserve banks, organised in a national network, and 24 branches, mainly involved in cheque clearing. The Fed sets reserve requirements for member banks, discount policy (the rate as lender of last resort), rates of interest that may be paid on sight or time deposits, and carries out open market operations – buying and selling government securities and bankers' acceptances. Members include all major US banks, who can borrow from the Fed at the discount rate or through repurchase agreements and use the Fed to clear cheques and make wire transfers.

Funds held by a bank in its reserve account at its local federal reserve bank are known as Fed funds and can be transferred through the Fed wire system around the country with same-day value. Fed funds provide the overnight market; other short-term funds are raised through repurchase agreements (repos), CDs, and commercial paper. Repos are the sale of a security, with a simultaneous agreement to repurchase the security at a future date, effectively a self-collateralising transaction.

The Fed takes a much more active role than the Bank of England in the way it supervises the banks it controls. Bank examiners regularly inspect the books of the banks, looking at the quality of their credit portfolios, as well as the efficiency of the banks' operations.

Prior to 1979, the US and UK authorities operated on very similar lines. Under those arrangements the Fed picked an appropriate level for the Fed funds rate, which it believed to be consistent with the attainment of its monetary targets. However, the Fed often proved slow in altering its federal funds rate intervention level in response to rising market rates. In consequence, it pumped out non-borrowed reserves and boosted monetary growth.

Since 1979, the Fed has sought directly to control the supply of bank reserves and to allow interest rates to find their own level. Like the Bank of England the Fed must relieve shortages of day-to-day credit (indeed the fact that banks hold reserves against deposits for an earlier period gives the Fed no option but to provide the reserves demanded by the system).

However, the way in which it acts is all important. The Fed seeks directly to control non-borrowed reserves. If these are in short supply the Fed funds rates will rise. Movements in the Fed funds rate will work their way through the US interest rate system. The direction of the Fed funds rate can be anticipated by the performance of money supply, normally announced on Friday afternoons.

Legal restrictions

Banking has always been fragmented in the US; in spite of 7,000 bank failures between 1929 and 1933, over 18,000 banks remained. There are today still over 12,000 separate banks in the US, due mainly to the Glass–Steagall Act which separates commercial banking from dealing in securities, a direct consequence of the Crash of 1929, and to the McFadden Act which restricts banking to certain areas. No bank is permitted to take deposits outside its home state; in some states it may only have one branch. By separate legislation banks are not allowed to pay more than 5 per cent for deposits.

These restrictions were introduced for good reasons, to safeguard depositors or to reduce monopoly situations and protect the savings and loan, or thrift, businesses. These laws are now outdated and most areas of the financial market are busy trying to change this legislation.

Nationwide banking is effected through the use of special vehicle subsidiaries such as the Edge Act companies, which may transact international trade, but may not take deposits.

Banking has developed within these legal constraints. While the basic business of borrowing and lending is similar to that in the UK, the use of overdrafts is unusual and most loans are on a formal basis, with fixed repayment dates. Banks price domestic loans on their prime rate, a rate calculated on short-term interest rates, or at a spread over prime. Fixed-term deposits are also a recent introduction. Borrowers are used to leaving balances with their banks to pay for services, particularly cash management services, to optimise having to use a large number of different banks to trade on a national basis.

Money markets

Development of the markets

Banks act as intermediaries between lenders and borrowers. Historically, the rates paid by banks for deposits have been kept low by regulation. This has led to two major waves of 'disintermediation', with investment banks or similar institutions taking business away from the commercial banking system.

The first wave was the development of the commercial paper market, in which corporations issue promissory notes for short periods, usually around one month, that provide cheap financing for the issuer and attractive returns for the investor buying the notes. The second development was the growth of money market funds offering the convenience of a savings account with much higher returns, giving small depositors access to higher interest rates through the pooling of their resources.

These changes in the market have led to a quite different structure when compared with the UK, with very large financial 'supermarkets' growing up in direct competition with the banking system. Combinations of commodity traders, investment banks and insurance companies are developing through a series of mergers and amalgamations. These anticipate the likely evolution of the commercial banks as the walls of legislation come down over the next few years.

There are two other major structural differences between the UK and the US financial markets. The first is the legislation preventing banks from dealing in securities, which has seen the growth of very large trading companies, investment banks and discount brokers, which provide liquidity through issuing bonds and commercial paper, and trade the paper that they issue, providing a deep secondary market. The second is the system of individual taxation, which is by negotiation between the taxpayer and the government, quite unlike the UK system of PAYE, where the taxpayer feels little incentive to be creative. There is consequently far more individual liquidity in the US and a very much wider range of instruments available, some quite specifically designed for complex, specialised tax situations.

Add to this the entrepreneurial nature of most Americans and the high level of trading in financial instruments will not come as a surprise. Companies such as Merrill Lynch have armies of salesmen distributing very complex financial products, selling individuals bonds, Treasury bills, CDs and other instruments, as well as the stocks and shares normally associated with a stockbroker.

With such a lot of money rolling on these financial instruments, the volatility and sharp upward rise in interest rates in 1980 brought the financial futures markets to life. Financial futures were new instruments that treated cash or securities as the commodities that they really are. It gave the punters a new market to speculate in and it gave the investor a means, albeit sometimes complex, to hedge against unexpected movements in the rates or prices affecting his investment. Merrill Lynch's salesmen quickly added futures to their product range.

All these activities, in the cash or the futures markets, are based on assumptions as to where the market is going in terms of interest rates. In the US this is controlled by the central bankers, the Fed, and its every pronouncement is analysed carefully for clues as to its future policies. Fed watching is a major pastime and fortunes are regularly gambled on the expected action that the Fed will take to meet the requirements of the US economy.

Eurodollars

Understanding the domestic money market is the key to forecasting future interest rate movements in the currency under consideration. Domestic markets exist in an international framework and are influenced by developments in other markets. The US dollar has always been an unrestricted currency and the ability to move dollars offshore led to the development of the Eurodollar market.

Shortly after the Second World War countries such as China and Russia began to hold their dollars outside the US to ensure that they could not be seized by the US Government. With the relaxation of financial controls many currencies became convertible into dollars and this, together with growing deficits in the US balance of payments, led to rapid growth of the market. The Eurodollar market finances countries and corporations and is of sufficient size to worry economists and politicians. The market is totally unregulated, and flows in and out of the market can be blamed for undermining the fiscal policies of individual countries.

Markets exist for several Eurocurrencies, but the dollar is dominant. The centre of the Euromarkets is in London, with other centres in Asia, Europe, the Caribbean and in International Banking Facilities in New York.

Eurodollars are used for two main types of financing, term loans with seven- to ten-year maturities, and Eurobonds with longer maturities. Large financings are usually split, or syndicated, among several lenders. These syndicated loans are often the major part of the international portfolios of many smaller sized banks.

The main international financial agencies, the Bank for International Settlements, International Monetary Fund and the World Bank, do not regulate the Euromarkets in any way, but exist to facilitate the international activities of central banks, to provide assistance to countries in economic distress and to channel aid to the Third World. This lack of regulation has its own benefits and it is unlikely that the world economy could have absorbed the oil shocks of the 1970s without the sponge of the Euromarkets to recycle the surpluses in the Middle East and finance the deficits of the Third World countries.

CHAPTER 9

Using money markets

The Euromarkets are the bridge between one national economy and another. That link is completed when we add foreign exchange to the equation. Before we look at foreign exchange in Chapter 10 we should examine in more detail the way money markets work.

Money markets are used when we need to borrow money or when we need to invest it. One person's loan is another person's investment. The borrower is concerned to raise loans at the lowest possible cost of funds, the lender to make the highest possible return on his investment. The credit standing of the borrower will affect the price of the loan, as will the degree of liquidity that the loan represents to the lender.

Borrowings can be made through trade financing (such as bankers' acceptances), non-fixed maturity products (such as overdrafts), fixed-rate loans for periods of one day to several years or loans on a floating rate basis where drawings are renewed from time to time at current market rates, with repayment due several years from the date of the original borrowing. Elaborate financings, such as Eurobonds, seek to give both borrowers and lenders the best of all possible worlds with regard to pricing and liquidity. Corporate borrowings tend to be by private arrangement; investments are usually made in standardised instruments.

Corporations looking to place surplus funds for a short period have a variety of instruments available, but in general place funds on call accounts or on short-term fixed deposits. Longer-term funds can be placed in a variety of instruments. The choice of how long the investment should be is determined by the company's forecast of future interest rates and possible tax considerations (for example, a chargeable capital gain may be preferable to income taxed at the corporation tax rate).

Yield curves

When interest rates are plotted against time they show what is known as a yield curve (see Fig. 9.1).

Interest rates traditionally were not volatile, with a 'normal' yield curve showing a tendency for rates to increase with time. Thus an overnight deposit would be priced at about, say, 1 per cent below a six-month deposit. The increase in rate represents the value of reinvesting the funds overnight

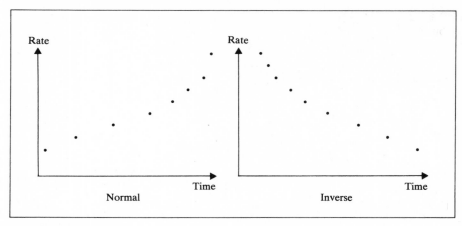

Fig. 9.1   Yield curves

(together with the overnight interest earned) for six months, assuming the overnight rate will not change for those six months. The rate will reflect the credit standing of the borrower (that is, the bank taking the deposit) and may also be adjusted by the borrower to take account of the perceived risk that interest rates may rise or fall during the life of the deposit. Expectation has an important impact on the shape of the yield curve. A steeply rising normal, or positive, yield curve indicates a market expectation of future increases in interest rates; a steeply falling yield curve (an inverse, or negative, yield curve) shows a general expectation of falling interest rates.

With a normal yield curve investors would look for longer-term instruments, with an inverse yield curve, short-term investments. Volatile interest rates can give rise to differently shaped curves, and to the appearance of both normal and inverse yield curves over a short time, but it is more likely for one type or the other to prevail for reasonably long periods.

The bond market

The bond market is a generic term used for fixed-rate investments. With the decline of the stock exchange as a way of raising long-term capital during the 1970s and early 1980s has come the growth of the bond market. Bonds issued by corporations are bought by creditors rather than investors and rank ahead of equity should the borrower be liquidated, an important consideration.

In the US there are three main types of bond issuers – the government, local government and corporations. Local government, or municipal, bonds have the lowest coupon (or interest) rates, as they are not subject to federal tax. Government bonds (themselves not subject to state tax) pay lower rates than corporations, as the credit is much stronger. Bonds dealt in the US can be issued in a variety of styles, such as convertible bonds or floating rate notes. Yankee bonds are issued by non-US entities and generally pay higher yields.

In the UK, the bond market is made up of government debt issues, gilts and the local authorities' issues. Continuing high inflation has effectively killed the market for corporate bonds.

Gilts are traded on The Stock Exchange in London and normally have a fixed coupon and redemption date. Gilts with a life of up to five years are known as short-dated, those with a life of five to ten years are medium-dated, and those with a life of at least ten years, but usually more than 15 years, are long-dated. Interest is paid semi-annually and gilts are traded with or without dividend interest. The government issues gilts by selling tap stock, where an issue of gilts is offered at a fixed price and yield (with any not taken up sold at a later date bit by bit by the government broker), and by tender, where the gilts are distributed to the highest bidders. Underwriting in the UK is not really practical, as the purchase of gilts by the banking sector would increase the money supply.

Gilts are dealt on The Stock Exchange by stockbrokers who execute buy or sell orders for their customers through stock jobbers. The government broker may intervene in the market, purchasing stocks approaching redemption or operating sinking funds. Yields are either fixed, variable or index-linked.

Eurobonds, as mentioned in Chapter 8, are debt instruments issued by borrowers outside their countries of residence, using the Euromarkets as an alternative source of liquidity.

The main fixed-rate sterling instruments are gilts, Treasury bills, sterling CDs, local authority paper, other government stocks and sterling Eurobonds (the 'Bulldog' market). Fixed-rate dollar instruments include dollar CDs, commercial paper, Treasury bills and bonds, other government paper and Eurobonds, which are also issued in a variety of other currencies.

The underlying value of a fixed-rate instrument is determined by the relationship between its fixed yield and prevailing interest rates. All fixed-rate instruments will rise in value if interest rates fall and will fall in value if interest rates rise. The price is adjusted to equate the value of the instrument at the fixed rate to the value of investing funds at today's rates.

Table 9.1 shows a list of the usual short-term facilities available to an investor.

Analysis of market data

Financial markets are characterised by an apparent complexity that reflects their rather haphazard development and the rapid rate of change in their structure and the products that are used or traded. Closer examination reveals that most of the relationships between different instruments can be expressed in terms of mathematical variables and that analysis of market data is no different from the analysis of any other type of information. Investment decisions in any of the instruments shown in Table 9.1 will be improved by using computer techniques to help implement and execute those decisions. The level of sophistication needed will depend on the way in which the user intends to use the markets. It would take a separate book to show in detail the mathematical and qualitative relationships that exist and must be understood to write the programs to manage the various financial instruments available.

Let us look at one simple example. We choose to buy a 90-day CD from a bank who issues it to us as a prime buyer. We have chosen to buy the CD because we value its liquidity and also because we feel that interest rates will fall. We value the liquidity because we may have to sell the CD in the secondary

Table 9.1   Short-term facilities

Facility	Return	Risk	Notes
Current accounts	None	Credit of bank	Some level of free balance may be needed to pay for services
Non-fixed deposit accounts	Below money market	Credit of bank	Call, composite, two- or seven-day notice
Time deposits	Near money market	Credit of bank; liquidity of deposit	Available one day to several years; may have to pay penalty to break early
CDs	Say 0.25% below money market	Credit of bank	Liquid instrument with possible capital gain if rates fall. Price depends on issuer's market status
Local authority bills	Say 0.125% below money market	Credit of the local authority	Up to one year (or longer). Negotiable instrument
Trade bills	Alternative forms of investment that may be attractive from time to time	Credit of issuer	Negotiable instrument
Bankers' acceptances		Credit of acceptor	Two name paper. Fully negotiable
Commercial paper and domestic bonds		Credit of issuer	Negotiable instruments
Eurobonds	Lower than deposit	Credit of issuer	Traded in mainly for capital gain, by investors looking for tax-free security and anonymity
Floating rate notes	On or over money market	Credit of issuer	Negotiable instruments
Gilts, treasury bills and bonds	Depends on market conditions	No credit risk, but may be liquidity risk	Need specialist advice before investing or entrusting others with investment
Commodities and financial futures		Speculative	
Stock market		Speculative. Liquidity	

market if we need the funds sooner than expected to pay for a known future obligation. We buy the CD for US $1,000,000 at a rate of 10 per cent. The only difference between a dollar and a sterling CD is that for calculation purposes all dollar transactions use a 360-day year, while sterling deals use a 365-day year. We can tell how much we will earn from the formula:

$$\text{Interest} = \frac{\text{Principal} \times \text{Coupon} \times \text{Days}}{36,000} = \frac{1,000,000 \times 10 \times 90}{36,000}$$

$$= \text{US\$25,000}$$

The CD is therefore worth US $1,025,000 at this time.

If we need to sell the CD in one month's time and rates have not changed, then the interest that the CD will earn will be:

$$\frac{1,000,000 \times 10 \times 60}{36,000} = \text{US \$16,666.67}$$

The purchaser should value the CD at US $1,016,666.67.

If we sell our CD, we will want to have reflected in the sale price a value for the interest earned so far. The price that would be paid will be calculated by comparing the values of the CD to the two parties:

$$\text{Price} = \text{Principal} \times \frac{\text{Old value of CD}}{\text{New value of CD}} = 1,000,000 \times \frac{1,025,000.00}{1,016,666.67}$$

$$= \text{US \$1,008,196.67}$$

We may have expected to receive one-third of the interest, US $8,333.33, but as the interest on the CD will not be collected until maturity, the price reflects the time value to the seller in getting his part of the interest immediately. We would follow the same steps if the interest rate had changed. Let us assume that the rate for a 60-day CD has fallen to 8 per cent after 30 days. The value of the 60-day CD is now:

$$\text{Principal} + \frac{1,000,000 \times 8 \times 60}{36,000} = \text{US \$1,013,333.33}$$

The price for the CD is therefore:

$$\text{Principal} \times \frac{1,025,000.00}{1,013,333.33} = \text{US \$1,011,513.10}$$

We have made US $(11,513.10 − 8,333.33), or US $3,179.77.

Each day that passes and each movement in the interest rates will affect the value of our CD. We will have to use a similar thought process in the evaluation of any borrowing or lending instrument. Measuring the impact of rate change on any position – cash, security or foreign exchange – is an important factor in money management.

All commercial enterprise is valued in terms of money and how that value changes over time. Suppose a manufacturer is concerned that the price of a commodity he uses will rise sharply. To protect himself he lays down a large stock of that commodity. At any time he can measure the effectiveness of his action by comparing the difference between the original and present prices of the commodity and the cost of borrowing the money needed to finance the purchase (or the value of the interest he could have earned by investing the money sensibly in the money market). Money should be viewed as a commodity and its time value is equally important to its owners.

Impact of rate movements

Information on interest rates is available from a variety of sources, including newspapers, TV, Reuters and other news services. Movements in rates are usually predictable on a day-to-day basis and while changing frequently during the day, do not have the same volatility as foreign exchange rates. Reuters and Telerate have extensive numbers of contributed pages of money market information. A typical Reuters page, giving Eurocurrency and domestic interest rates, is shown in Fig. 9.2.

```
1431      EDD - FRANKFURT TEL 611 20671 TX 414238              EDDD
DEPOSITS    US DOLLAR        D MARK      DM DOMESTIC    RENDITE
 1 MTH     9 3/8-1/2       5 9/-11/16    5.70-80     1 YEAR    6.75T
 2 MTHS    9 7/-9/16       5 5/8-3/4     5.75-80     2 YEARS   7.30T
 3 MTHS    9 9/-11/16      5 13/-15/16   5.75-85     3 YEARS   7.90T
 6 MTHS    9 11/-13/16     5 7/8-6.00    6.20-30     4 YEARS   8.20T
 9 MTHS    9 7/8-10.00     6 1/8-1/4     6.45-55     5 YEARS   8.34T
12 MTHS    10.00-1/8       6 3/-5/16     6.65-75     6 YEARS   8.40T
 2 YEARS   10 7/8-1/8      7.00-1/4      7.40-70     7 YEARS   8.40T
 3 YEARS   11 1/8-3/8      7 3/4-8.00    7.95-25     8 YEARS   8.40T
 4 YEARS   11 1/2-3/4      8 1/8-3/8     8.20-50     9 YEARS   8.45T
 5 YEARS   11 3/4-12.00    8 3/8-5/8     8.35-65    10 YEARS   8.50T
```

Fig. 9.2   A typical Reuters page (Eurocurrency and domestic interest rates)

The bank lends at the higher rate and borrows at the lower rate. Similar screens show the rates for money market instruments. A screen provided by a London broker shows the rates for sterling instruments that applied at about the same time as the EDDD screen shown above (see Fig. 9.3).

```
1418 ASTLEY AND PEARCE LONDON - STERLING    * EURO STERLING ASPS
     INTER BANK - 01 623 3391  -  CDS       *          TX 897065
O/N 9 1/2    1/4      1   9 23/32   21/32   VALUE 3 OCTOBER
W/F 9 7/8    3/4      2   9 9/16.   17/32   1M  9 11/16       5/8
1   9 3/4    11/16    3   9 15/32   13/32   2M  9 11/16       9/16
2   9 5/8    9/16     4   9 7/16    13/32   3M  9 5/8         1/2
3   9 5/8    1/2      5   9 7/16    13/32   6M  9 5/8         9/16
4   9 5/8    1/2      6   9 7/16    13/32   1Y  9 15/16      13/16
5   9 5/8    9/16     7   9 17/32   15/32   ******************
6   9 5/8    9/16     8   9 9/16    1/2     CDS CONTINUED
9   9 7/8    3/4      9   9 19/32   17/32   11  9 5/8   9/16
12  9 15/16  13/16   10   9 5/8     9/16    12  9 5/8   9/16
```

Fig. 9.3   Rates for sterling instruments

If we want to compare the sterling rates with the dollar or Deutschmark rates then we must take into account the relative value of the currencies and we will discuss the way to do this in Chapter 10. However, we cannot always directly compare the rates between one instrument and another in the same currency, as the means of quoting that rate are not always the same. This is particularly true of debt instruments, such as bankers' acceptances, that are quoted on a discount rather than a yield basis.

While CDs are obviously bought for their yield, the purchaser is always prepared to surrender some of that yield for the liquidity that the instrument provides. Thus the sterling CD rates in Fig. 9.3 show the instrument trading at 0.062 per cent ($^1/_{16}$) less for one month, 0.187 per cent ($^3/_{16}$) less for six months and 0.312 per cent ($^5/_{16}$) less for one year. Secondary CDs are traded at prices that reflect the current interest rates; as interest rates rise the price of the CD falls and the opposite happens if rates fall. The price is calculated by a reasonably complex series of formulae, a process that lends itself admirably to computer analysis. Each instrument shown in Table 9.1 has peculiarities in the way it is priced and quoted and the depth of liquidity in the market may also be an important determinant in the way rates are derived.

The money market instruments are all speciality products that reflect the credit standing of the issuer and offer opportunities for arbitrage, whereby profits can be gained without taking risk. A bank has to manage its interest rate position within the constraints of its balance sheet and its ability to increase its capital to support its asset base, which is mostly in the form of risk assets – loans to customers or for money market activities. For every asset there must be a liability, so that the bank must fund its loan portfolio; conversely every deposit must be offset by a loan to a customer or a participant in the money market. If assets and liabilities are mismatched, the bank is said to be gapping, or taking a position against the prevailing yield curve, and taking a risk that incremental profit can be taken from that position.

Let us assume that a bank has the position shown in Table 9.2.

Table 9.2   A sample position

Time category	Assets (US$m)	Liabilities (US$m)	Gap
Non-fixed	50	220	170
One month	50	225	175
Three months	150	30	−120
Six months	200	25	−175
One year +	100	50	−50
	550	550	

If the average rate for the assets is higher than the average rate paid for liabilities then the bank will make a profit, providing that rates do not change over time. Let us ascribe some interest rates to Table 9.2 (see Table 9.3).

Table 9.3   Gapping income

Time category	Assets (US$m)	Average rate (%)	Liabilities (US$m)	Average rate (%)
Non-fixed	50	10	220	10
One month	50	10	225	10
Three months	150	11	30	11
Six months	200	12	25	12
One year +	100	12	50	12
	550	11.4	550	10.3

The 1.1 per cent difference between the income from assets and the cost of liabilities represents earnings of $5.95 million on a balance sheet with footings of $550 million. If the interest rates for non-fixed maturity and one-month assets and liabilities go up by 2 per cent then the overall cost of total liabilities will rise to 11.9 per cent, while the income from total assets will grow at a slower rate to 11.7 per cent; this would create a loss of $1.2 million. A movement of this sort is neither violent nor unusual by money market standards.

To remove its timing risk the bank has to increase its balance sheet by US $345 million; this could put strain on the bank's capital adequacy. The bank may choose not to correct the temporal mismatch, but if it takes that decision it needs to know the financial risk that it is taking at all times and the cost of eliminating that risk by intelligently comparing the value of its balance sheet with current interest rates.

When a company's reputation is damaged its liquidity is also threatened. It finds it more difficult to raise finance and cannot sell its investments at market rates. The same is true of banks, as was seen when the failure of Penn Square led to the downgrading of the credit rating of several other banks, most noticeably Continental Illinois, who then had to pay substantially more for its funds for a period of several months. A run on liquidity followed, forcing Continental to seek government protection, which it may need for several years before it can stand on its own feet again.

Banks are now using the financial futures markets to manage their interest rate bets without their having an impact on their balance sheets. Financial futures extend the techniques of commodity trading to the financial markets and are particularly useful in interest rate hedging and, to a lesser extent, for foreign exchange. As with other financial instruments, the basic calculations are complex and the interaction of the cash and futures markets creates a further area for arbitrage and speculation.

Treasury managers have to know their interest rate positions at all times and this includes the treasurers of non-bank companies. Whereas banks suffer greatly if they make the wrong interest rate bet, a manufacturing company, with only a relatively small proportion of its balance sheet in liquid form, is usually more concerned with the opportunity profit or loss that funding decisions will lead to.

CHAPTER 10

Foreign exchange

Foreign exchange is the means by which money moves from one currency into another to pay for imports, exports or capital investments. The foreign exchange markets are used to convert one currency into another, both for immediate and for future requirements, and to hedge or reduce the risk associated with trade flows or assets denominated in a foreign currency. This chapter describes these markets and the factors that affect foreign rates and composite currencies, such as the ECU and the SDR, and discusses the elements of how to deal in foreign exchange.

Size and main functions of the markets

The dimensions of the foreign exchange markets are not documented and therefore difficult to determine. No one really knows, but with world trade totalling about US $2,000 billion a year, a reasonable estimate would put the volume of foreign exchange traded at about US $40,000 billion. Trade-related foreign exchange represents no more than 3 per cent of the total foreign exchange market, with the rest of the volume coming from banks dealing among themselves. The total market is therefore about US $10 billion a day, split roughly between London, with 30 per cent of the volume; West Germany, 25 per cent; Switzerland, 17 per cent; the US, 12 per cent; the Middle and Far East, 9 per cent; and the rest of Europe, 7 per cent. With the dollar on one side of every transaction, the main trading currencies are the Deutschmark, with 40 per cent of volume; Swiss franc, 18 per cent; sterling, 15 per cent; French franc, 5 per cent; yen, 5 per cent; Canadian dollar, 5 per cent; Dutch guilder, 5 per cent; and other currencies, 8 per cent.

Eighty per cent of all trading is in spot deals for delivery in the next two working days; most forward deals are interbank swaps. The amount of forward dealing appears to have been reduced due to rate uncertainty in the last few years and banks now concentrate on very short-term positions that can be liquidated at minimal cost.

Even with the predominance of interbank dealing, the fundamental cause of all foreign exchange is to satisfy the needs of international commercial activities or investments, particularly the financing of commodity trading. These commercial transactions tend to be the prime movers of the markets in terms of demand and rate movement. The foreign exchange markets are so large and so liquid that no single participant can influence them for anything other than a very short period and then only at times of quiet trading.

Foreign exchange and balance of payments

Foreign exchange transactions involve the currencies of at least two different countries. These movements have an impact on the balance of payments of the countries concerned. A central bank may protect its balance of payments by imposing measures, such as exchange controls, to limit the convertibility of its currency into others. These controls are usually intended to limit speculation without reducing the flow of genuine commercial transactions. European countries with rigid exchange controls include France and Sweden.

Exchange rates now float freely or are confined within a floating system such as the EMS. They are therefore sensitive to a range of factors. One of the most important is the country's balance of payments account. Put simply, the balance in a country's reserves will be affected by movements in the current balance and the capital balance. The current balance is the difference between the value of exports of goods and services and the value of imports of goods and services, while the capital balance is the difference between long-term inflows and outflows, both private and official. If the sum of the current balance and capital balance movements in a given period is positive, then there has been an increase in the country's reserves; if it is negative, then there has been a decrease. If that decrease is repeated, eventually reserves will become insufficient to meet obligations. A decrease in reserves is likely then to weaken the exchange rate and its future expectations.

Forecasting future trends

Each country will need an individual analysis to see what may happen to its currency. Thus a country relying heavily on tourism to boost its export of services may be severely affected by civil disturbances or bad weather. Exchange rate weakness can be caused by government overborrowing or overspending overseas and weakness will increase speculation or the leading or lagging, the speeding up or slowing down of payments settling trade flows, which can have a significant impact on day-to-day demand. A country with a high inflation rate will see its currency progressively devalue against the currency of another country with a lower inflation rate. Thus it is important to watch indicators of inflation, such as the retail price index, as a guide for the future.

The participants in the market make assumptions as to the likely future impact of important indicators such as these. Movements in exchange or interest rates will reflect these expectations which occasionally may have greater short-term impact than can be justified by the underlying economic trends. Should that be the case, then usually a reaction will set in which will restore the exchange rate or interest rate to reflect the true position.

When large numbers of people anticipate a change in an exchange rate, then activity in dealings in the currency concerned will increase. This activity will come from speculation and from companies entering hedging transactions to protect themselves from the expected exchange rate movement. If the expectation is one of devaluation there will be increased interest in selling the currency outright for a forward date. The forward premium will only get out of line with interest differentials if there is a market imperfection, such as exchange controls. The central bank concerned is likely to be closely involved with this activity, although, historically, central banks have been able to do little other than change the timing of a determined trend in the market.

Forecasting future foreign exchange or interest rates is carried out by two main schools, fundamental economists and technical analysts. The former apply generally held economic theories to predict future exchange or interest rates. Technical analysts derive information from plotting movements in exchange or interest rates and predicting the future by extrapolation from the patterns on the chart or by the mathematical fitting of a curve to those patterns. Fundamental economists need periods of economic stability to be most effective and are probably most successful and most useful in predicting the development of long-term trends, particularly in times of significant movements in rates.

Types of foreign exchange contracts

Obtaining information

This section looks at the different types of foreign exchange contracts used on a daily basis by participants in the markets. Information on market rates and trends can be obtained from banks or other major users of the market, the usual news media, such as newspapers or television, or from Reuters, Telerate or other news services. The *Financial Times* provides the most complete newspaper coverage of the financial markets; the information is of course of historical interest only and is occasionally misleading and care should be exercised in relating rates shown in the newspaper to dealing rates that took place in the market at that time.

Reuters and Telerate information is provided by the banks themselves through complex electronic link-ups with central computers which belong to the news services. Information always therefore suffers some delay before appearing on the screen and these delays will increase if the markets are busy, as often it is the position dealer who keeps his currency up to date on his bank's information page. In Fig. 10.1 is shown a typical Reuter's page: we will use this information to derive spot and forward exchange rates in the rest of this chapter.

```
0000    CITIBANK EUROPE FOREIGN EXCHANGE RATES - PAGE          CITX


              SPOT        1 MONTH   2 MONTHS   3 MONTHS   6 MONTHS
1433 DM       2.6470/80     87/82    177/172    255/250    497/487
1418 STG      1.4965-75      3/0      -2/+2        5/9       21/26
1430 SF       2.1350/60    102/97    200/195    283/278    547/537
1428 YEN      236.80-90     57/52    117/112    178/173    370/360
1424 FF       8.0325/50    220/260   570/630   1000/1075  2350/2450 X
1420 LIT      1604.10/60  1200/1300 2300/2500  3400/3600  6725/7125
1422 DFL      2.9600-10     90/87    172/168    250/246    488/482
1431 BFC      53.655/665    -2/+1     -1/+3       00/5        5/11
1432 DKR      9.5565/90    -35/+15   -40/+10     35/85     125/225
1432 ASH      18.6140/90   600/525  1250/1050  1750/1500  3100/2750
0000
```

Fig. 10.1   A typical Reuters page (foreign exchange rates)

This particular Reuters screen uses the special features of Reuters quite extensively. Each line is entered by the European branch which is the major market maker for the bank in Europe. Thus Frankfurt enters the Deutschmark line; Zurich, the Swiss franc; London, the cable (US dollar/sterling) and the yen, and because there is no forward market in Paris, London provides the rates for forward French francs. The left-hand column is a time stamp that alters each time an element of information in that line changes. Each information provider has a different method of collecting and presenting information and users should be aware of these differences, so that they can evaluate the worth of individual rate screens.

Bid and offer prices

In foreign exchange, rates are quoted as 'bid', the price at which the quoting party is prepared to purchase a currency, or 'offer', the price at which it sells the currency. Thus the bid for one currency is also the offer for the other currency involved. In interbank dealing, the bid rate normally refers to the purchase of US dollars, the offer rate to the sale of US dollars.

To give an example, for an exchange between Deutschmark (DM) and US dollars the rate is quoted as 2.6470/2.6480 (see Table 10.1).

Table 10.1   An exchange between Deutschmarks and US dollars

Bid	*Offer*
Bank buys US dollars	Bank sells US dollars
Bank sells Deutschmarks	Bank buys Deutschmarks
2.6470	2.6480
Customer sells US dollars	Customer buys US dollars
Customer buys Deutschmarks	Customer sells Deutschmarks

With sterling, which is quoted in units of dollars, the bid and offered prices would be the reverse of the examples shown in Table 10.1 (see Table 10.2).

Table 10.2   Bid and offered prices of sterling

Bid	*Offer*
Bank buys sterling	Bank sells sterling
Bank sells US dollars	Bank buys US dollars
1.4965	1.4975
Customer sells sterling	Customer buys sterling
Customer buys US dollars	Customer sells US dollars

This would apply to other currencies, such as the Australian dollar, which is also quoted in terms of units of US dollars per unit of currency.

To make a profit, the bank tries to sell as little currency as possible for each US dollar and to buy as much currency as possible for each US dollar.

Cross rates

Most foreign exchange is contracted against the US dollar. Thus if a bank wishes to convert Deutschmarks into sterling then it effects a Deutschmark/US dollar transaction, offset by a US dollar/sterling deal. Cross rates are calculated by using simple rules.

1.   In Europe all foreign exchange rates are quoted in terms of currency units per US $1, with the exception of sterling, Irish punts, Australian dollars, New Zealand dollars and South African rand, which are quoted in terms of US dollars per one currency unit. This convention is widespread and has for the most part replaced the practice in the US where rates were quoted as reciprocals of the European rates (that is, in terms of the US dollars/currency unit).

2.   Thus we can establish two groups of major currencies.

Group A	Group B
Sterling, Irish punts, Australian dollars, New Zealand dollars, South African rand	All other major currencies

3.   Within each group of currencies, divide the 'larger' number by the 'smaller'. Therefore, to sell Deutschmarks for French francs, the bank needs to calculate 8.0325/2.6470 = 3.0346 French francs per DM 1. Note that the bank has effectively sold US dollars for French francs and bought US dollars for Deutschmarks to create the cross rate, although US dollars will not be paid or received in the settlement of the transaction.

4.   To establish the cross rate between a currency in Group A with one in Group B, multiply the two rates together. Thus, to sell sterling and buy Deutschmarks the bank has to calculate 1.4975 × 2.6480 = 3.9654. The opposite deal would be effected at 1.4965 × 2.6470 = 3.9612, so that the cross rate for sterling/Deutschmark is 3.9612/3.9654.

Spot and forward transactions

The spot rate normally has a value date set as the second working day after the date on which the transaction is concluded. Thus a spot deal made on a Thursday will be settled the following Monday or the next business day if that Monday is a holiday. The forward dates are by convention set by adding calendar months to the spot date or taken to the next business day if the forward date falls on a weekend or a holiday. Thus a three-month deal will cover a varying number of days, depending on when the deal is struck. To obtain a 90-day rate may require some small adjustment to the three-month rate. For a transaction made on 20 April 1984 the forward dates would be as shown in Table 10.3.

Table 10.3   Sample forward dates

Transaction day		Settlement date
20 April 1984	Spot	24 April 1984 (Easter intervenes)
	One month	24 May 1984
	Two months	25 June 1984 (24 June is a Sunday)
	Three months	24 July 1984
	Six months	24 September 1984

If the spot value is the last working day of the month, then the forward value automatically becomes the last working day when forward rates are quoted for whole months, for example, for a spot value of 31 January 1984 the one month forward date would be 29 February 1984.

Forward rates are shown as points that represent the interest rate differential between one Eurocurrency and another. These forward points are quoted as differentials, expressed as premiums or discounts, and are shown for various periods on the Reuters screen. The outright forward rate is found by adding premiums to or subtracting discounts from the spot rate. Forward rates fluctuate less often than spot rates, due mainly to the slower speed of change of interest rates experienced in the money market. The simple purchase of a currency on a fixed future date is known as a forward outright deal.

In the example shown in Table 10.4 the base currency is the US dollar; we define the base currency as the currency against which other currencies are quoted. If we go back to our split of currencies into Group A and Group B, then Group A currencies would always be base currencies, while within Group B the US dollar will always be the base currency. Quite simply, at any particular time the buying price of the base currency will always be lower than the selling price. For the three-month US dollar/Deutschmark and the three-month US dollar/Italian lira bid and offer prices see Table 10.4.

Table 10.4   Three-month bid and offer prices

Deutschmarks	Bid (US $)	Offer (US $)	Lira	Bid (US $)	Offer (US $)
Spot	2.6470	2.6480	Spot	1604.1	1604.6
Points (three months) US dollar discount, so subtract	0.0255	0.0250	Points (three months) US dollar premium, so add	34.0	36.0
	2.6215	2.6230		1638.1	1640.6

Adding or subtracting by mistake will always make it cheaper to sell the currency than to buy it. If the forward points on the lira had been subtracted rather than added, that is, treated as a US dollar discount rather than a US dollar premium, then the forward bid and offer rates would have been 1,570.10 and 1,568.60 and the buying price for US dollars higher than the selling price for US dollars. Note that the difference between the bid and offer widens to cover the additional risk underlying the forward transaction.

As mentioned earlier, the forward points represent the difference in interest rates between one currency and another. Thus, for US dollars/Deutschmarks the three-month differential would be the annualised points' difference as a percentage of the spot rate.

$$\frac{0.0255 \times 4 \times 100}{2.6470} = 3.853\%$$

This is a simplified formula which gives a reasonable approximation. The currency with the numerically higher interest rate will be at a discount to a currency with a lower interest rate and conversely the currency with the lower interest rate is at a premium to a currency with a higher rate of interest.

Three-month Eurodollars should yield around 3.8 per cent more than the three-month Euro-Deutschmarks in the example shown above; if this was not the case, then speculators would arbitrage the forward market and very quickly cause the forward points to come into line. A more accurate calculation (substituting the number of days in the formula for the number of months) shows a difference of yield of 3.77 per cent, in comparison with the difference of 3.75 per cent shown on the EDDD screen in Fig. 10.1. The EDDD and CITX screens were printed off within a few minutes of each other: the 0.02 per cent differential may or may not exist and can only be confirmed by getting rates out of the market. Reuters, Telerate and other information sources do not necessarily quote the prevailing rate, due to the lag caused by getting information into the network, and it should not be surprising if rates quoted by dealers differ from those on the screen.

When calculating forward prices it is possible to apply some fundamental, but practical, rules of thumb. If the left-hand side of the forward rate is greater than the right-hand side, points are subtracted; if the right-hand side is the larger, then points are added to the spot rate. As a check, the sum of the difference between the spot bid and offer rates and the forward bid and offer points will equal the difference between the forward outright bid and offer rates. Thus for Deutschmark/US dollar, spot rates are 2.6470/2.6480 and the one-month adjustment 87/82 outrights are calculated as 2.6470–2.0087 and 2.6480–2.0082, giving forward rates of 2.6383/2.6398, a spread of 15 points (ten from spot, five from the forward points).

Let us do two more rate computations and buy six-month sterling for yen and three-month Belgian francs for Deutschmarks. The calculations are as follows.

Sterling/yen, six-month $(236.9 - 3.6) \times (1.4975 + 0.0026) = 349.97$

Belgian francs/Deutschmarks, three-month $- \dfrac{(53.655 + 0)}{(2.6480 - 0.0250)} = 20.456$

Swap transactions

A swap is effected by the purchase of one currency in exchange for another on a given date, simultaneously reversed by the sale of the first currency for the second on a different maturity date. There is no cash flow in a swap, as the currency bought on the spot date is replaced by the currency sold on the forward date. Thus, it is the swap points that are important and the spot rate is relatively unimportant, as long as it reflects closely the prevailing market prices. Thus, if a customer wishes to enter into a one-month swap by buying sterling spot for dollars and reversing the transaction on the forward date, he will earn three forward points. The bank may choose to alter the spot rate to 1.4967 to give a forward rate of 1.4970 for ease of calculation.

A more complex swap would be for a six-month deal between French francs and sterling, with the customer buying the French francs on the spot date.

Calculate spot rate: $8.0350 \times 1.4975 = 12.0324$
Calculate six-month rate: $8.2800 \times 1.5001 = 12.4208$

The French franc/sterling swap rate is therefore 3,884 points. The swap rate represents the interest differential between two currencies. Swaps are therefore used to hedge cross currency positions in the money market or to lock in exchange rates to ensure a required rate of interest on a loan or deposit in a foreign currency.

Interbank trading

Foreign exchange dealing is a repetitive business that is made difficult by the continuous changes in the market and the need to judge the best time to deal in order to take advantage of anticipated movements in rates. This is fine as long as your anticipation is correct. A bank has to make a price for the currencies it trades in whenever it is called by a customer or a counterparty in the interbank market. If it is late in the day or the markets are really unsettled, then a bank may be allowed to decline to quote; such an action at other times could see the bank having problems in placing its own business with its counterparties at a later time. The market works on reciprocity.

Most banks have a team of dealers available to help customers use the markets, to give advice and execute transactions in the foreign exchange and deposit markets. One of the roles of the customer dealer should be to protect the customer from prices that reflect the bank's position to the detriment of the customer; he therefore needs access to a wide range of sources of market information.

The principles of interbank trading are quite simple. A bank looks at the rates in a completely opposite way to its customer. Let us suppose that we are the Deutschmark dealer, and that prevailing foreign exchange rates are those shown in Table 10.1.

Let us suppose that we are the Deutschmark dealer. We have no opinion about the way the market is going, so that we have a completely square position. A customer or another bank calls us and asks to sell us US $1,000,000.00 for Deutschmarks. We buy the US dollars at 2.6470 and now are long on US dollars and short on Deutschmarks. In other words, we have a position that we may not want to have, as we were trying to keep square. We want to sell US $1,000,000.00 and buy DM 2,647,000 to get out of the position.

If rates have not changed and we call another bank immediately, we now become that bank's customer and can transact at 2.6470. We have neither gained nor lost, but over time this type of dealing would cause us to go bankrupt, as we are not covering our transaction costs, let alone the cost of the dealers and the overhead that they carry. However, if the other bank has a position or an expectation, it will change the rate to reflect its thinking. It may quote us 2.6465–2.6475, and we will lose DM 500 on the deal. Rates move around the whole time as dealers make prices, take profits and settle positions throughout the day. Of course if someone else calls us and wants to buy US £1,000,000.00 for Deutschmarks, then we will quote him 2.6465–2.6475 to show our keenness to buy Deutschmarks; if he deals we clear DM 500 for ourselves.

A busy interbank dealer handles around 300 deals a day in a major currency such as the Deutschmark; keeping track of his position is a major headache.

Many large companies have their own dealers. While the company may cover every foreign exchange requirement as it comes up it will always have a foreign exchange exposure of some kind if it is involved in foreign trade or has overseas subsidiaries. We will look in Chapters 13, 14 and 15 at how banks and corporations manage these problems.

CHAPTER 11

Dealing room technology

The most active users of the money and foreign exchange markets are the major commercial banks who act as clearing centres for their customers (including other banks), matching buyers to sellers, usually indirectly by taking their customers' orders directly into their positions.

A bank's treasury is usually made up of a group of dealers, who generate large volumes of transactions in the financial markets. The dealers are supported by operations staff who process the deals, usually by entering the information on a hand-written deal ticket into a terminal which feeds a mainframe computer serving the whole bank or for a large treasury, into a minicomputer which serves the treasury and gives information to the mainframe.

The dealers have counterparties who may be introduced by brokers or may be direct customers of the bank. One main concern is with the credit standing of these counterparties and the amount of credit line that is available.

Once he has entered a transaction the dealer needs to know his position, which as we have seen is a critical factor in the way he prices his bids and offers. He needs to be able to calculate rates quickly, see what is happening in the world through Reuters or Telerate and communicate immediately with his brokers and major customers.

Two of the most active banks in London are Chase Manhattan and Citibank. Both are major international banks and play important roles in the interbank markets. In addition, both specialise in the provision of treasury products to their corporate customers. This chapter mainly looks at how these two banks manage their treasury operations. Of particular interest is the investment that Chase has made in modern dealing room technology and the way Citibank has gone about automating the dealing process.

An example of dealing room technology

The Chase Manhattan dealing room in London, opened in August 1983, contains the latest in modern communications and dealing environment technology. Its treasury dealing room is both a hub of financial activities and a showpiece for the bank's customers – the treasury is after all one of the few places in a bank that looks busy and bustling. The dealing room takes up most of one floor and has been designed to let dealers see as much as possible of what is going on in other parts of the room. The dealing desks are made from dark, expensive-looking wood and are arranged in crescent shapes, with the dealers all facing into the centre of the room. The lighting is very effective, giving an impression of almost sombre calm, yet providing very high quality illumination in every working area.

The dealers have the most modern electronic equipment, much of it connected through cables made from optical fibres, which reduce the sheer bulk of cabling needed for conventional wires. Access to all its computer-generated data as well as external news sources is through a Reuters programmable keyboard, which switches between one screen and another at the push of a button. Dealers have access to their own computer facility to generate rate information or to take information formatted off a Reuters feed to their computer. Voice communications with the outside world are made through British Telecom's City Business System, with calls dialled and connected through a touch of the screen. Telex machines are the latest style, with memories, screens and word processing facilities, as well as simplified dial procedures to make connections with branches and other banks as rapid as possible.

While Chase has provided its dealers certainly with one of the most attractive dealing rooms in London, it has not yet properly addressed the interface between the dealers and the computer when it comes to deal and transaction processing. It is a question of managerial philosophy as to which is more important: having the dealer control and take full responsibility for his actions or delegating that responsibility to the operational department processing the transactions, including the timely presentation of positional information. In spite of all their computerisation, the dealers in Chase still complete deal slips and thus perpetuate the multiple input of information that can be easily avoided by using modern technology.

Special accounting and reporting systems

Most banks have had to add special accounting and reporting systems for their trading activities in foreign exchange and money markets as the growth in this business accelerated over the past ten years and their basic book-keeping systems could not keep up. Many have bought software packages from specialist companies, of which the best known are BIS, with its Midas system, and CDC with Arbat. These provide so-called front-end systems to the dealing room and are based on a microcomputer which sits between the treasury operation and the bank's mainframe. Dealers fill in deal slips and pass them to be enhanced and entered by support clerks. A reasonable degree of automation exists with regard to generating confirmations and preparing positional information from the clerical input. Transactional information is then passed to the back office and more details added to cover charges, to pay and receive instructions and the like.

Where these systems 'score' is in the provision of dealers' aids. Pages are generated either from the dealers' own rate inputs or from information services such as Reuters and presented quickly and conveniently to the dealer. The same keyboard is usually used to perform these functions, as well as to get into the mainframe for transactional details and to view the reported position on the bank's books.

Dealer support tends to concentrate on the provision of rate information rather than absolutely up-to-date positional information, which after all has to be put in by clerks who have to serve several dealers at the same time. Dealers therefore have to rely on their memories or on hand-written blocks, both dangerous things in a highly volatile and fragmented business environment.

An alternative approach

An alternative approach is to make the dealer totally responsible for all his activities, with safeguards built in by monitoring his decisions. As the markets become more and more frantic, the less reliance that there is on keeping positions on manual blocks, the better the decision-making process. With all their other pressures it is unreasonable to expect operational departments to present positional information instantly, as soon as a deal has been transacted, which is when the dealer needs to know.

Another new dealing room, opened by Bank of America in Los Angeles towards the end of 1983, incorporates technology designed to solve this problem. The 32 dealers sit in front of work-stations which incorporate six different video screens, two of which are colour monitors linked to an IBM-PC dedicated to the work-station. Using an electronic pen, the dealer enters transactional information into his computer which is networked to the other dealing stations, central servers and a hard disc which provides memory storage. This method of data entry has been formulated from an early version of the dealer support system developed by Citibank in its treasury operation in London. This dealing system, known as Cititrader, demonstrates one of the best examples of how to use small computers to boost productivity in a financial institution.

Cititrader began in 1980 more as a series of happy coincidences than as the result of any grand plan. A senior dealer, later to become head trader in the interbank foreign exchange room, had a background in computer studies. He felt that there had to be an easier way to keep positions in foreign exchange than the traditional means – writing on a scruffy piece of paper with a leaking pen – and so he wrote an embryonic program to keep positions on an Apple microcomputer. At about this time most of the senior managers in London were being subjected to intensive training in technology. One of these managers was the then treasurer, who had just discovered that an Apple was more than a typewriter and quickly grasped the potential of the position keeping system.

It was decided to use the position keeper for all the foreign exchange dealers and a small technology unit was formed to develop it. The initial systems were held on stand-alone Apples, which kept up to six different currencies, both spot and forward. With the exception of sterling, the biggest currency in terms of volume and numbers of transactions, each position was managed in the same way from a book-keeping point of view. The forward cable dealer required a different screen format and a special adaptation of the program was used.

Dealers wrote out the bare minimum of information on a deal ticket, passed the ticket to operational support personnel, who enhanced the deal ticket and entered the deal information on to the keyboard of the Apple II position keeper. The deal ticket was then passed through to the back office, where it was destined to be keyed at least two more times to get it on to the mainframe computer. The support personnel worked in the dealing room alongside the dealers; the positions created by their inputs of data were shown on screens in front of the dealers. At this stage, six months into the development, position keeping increased the daily workload in the dealing room, but the gains in profitability amply rewarded the cost of the extra effort.

Market conditions have become more frantic over the past few years and the volatility of intra-day trading makes it essential for the dealer to have up-to-date information at all times. This was difficult, given the various tasks facing the support personnel, not least of which was deciphering the dealers' handwriting. The growing volume of transactions coming out of the customer dealers, who were established in a separate dealing room, often led to delays in entering deals on the position keepers. It was decided to experiment with direct deal input by the dealers and then to create a network of Apples to provide many of the support functions needed by the dealers.

It was well known throughout the dealing community in London that input through a keyboard would not be fast enough for a dealer and would cause too much clutter on his desk. By using a graphics tablet and electronic stylus to input data, probably the first time this had ever been done, it was possible for the dealer to enter quite complex deal details in a matter of a few presses of the electronic pen. Use of this technique also removed the stigma of being an input clerk, whose work a dealer associated with keyboard entry. The success of the experiment was such that the decision was taken to go ahead quickly and the first networked system was in place and working within two years of producing the first program. Dealers are now supported by networked Apples, which converse with each other or with special application Apples through a ribbon cable. Within the network is a central memory and backup memory which house the programs that run the systems.

The dealer's Apple is actually in his desk and several networks are used, based on Zynar's Cluster One, with a large disc used to store programs and output from the dealers' Apples in a central place. Apples are able to communicate with each other through the network and also with special applications Apples that produce positional information through to the bank's mainframe. The dealer views the information produced on the same screens he uses to view his Reuters and Telerate services, as well as the bank's other computer systems. The dealer is surrounded by communications equipment and the dealer system is just one of several activities he must monitor.

A key feature of the introduction of these systems has been the user's involvement. Each dealer is extensively consulted before a new system is installed and no dealer is obliged to use the system if it does not satisfy him. The extent to which Apple-based systems are used throughout the dealing rooms, by funding and customer dealers, as well as interbank foreign exchange traders, is a measure of user satisfaction. Direct dealing has released dealers or support staff from the onerous task of calculating book-keeping entries, permitting impressive gains in productivity. Further efficiencies arise from passing transactional data directly from the Apple network to the first level of back office computers in the operational support group.

Citibank's London treasury now has six Apple networks, including two for development. Its new, enlarged dealing room will be completed during 1984 and each of the 56 dealing positions will have an Apple dedicated to it. In addition, there are another 30 Apples performing specialised tasks or held on stand-by in case of malfunction. The efficiency of the network has been quite remarkable and the 'downtime' on the Apples much less than expected. One of the benefits of the distributed processing approach is that the part of the system most likely to go down, the microprocessor, is not a critical element, as the dealer's position can be quickly recreated from the central memory. The dealer never loses more than the deal he is working on, as he can move to another desk and pick up where he left off while he waits for the Apple to be quickly replaced – in a matter of a few minutes he can be back at his own desk.

Not least of the advantages has been the improved ability of management to interact with the dealers in a constructive manner. Traditionally, the only person who knew what was going on during the day was the interbank dealer himself and he resented being continually checked on, particularly if he was not doing very well. Conversations with management could be tense in these circumstances, with most of the time spent on determining just what the position actually was. With the computerised dealing system, the treasurer can see the positions that his traders have taken without having to walk about the room and ask what may be embarrassing questions, as he is also connected to the network and can watch the activity in the market without having to leave his office. Discussions can concentrate on deciding what to do next rather than having to continually ask 'where are we now?' or 'how are you doing?'

The system is described below in some of the applications used in the London treasury, where there are different adaptations for spot and forward foreign exchange dealers, customer foreign exchange dealers (who place all transactions through the interbank dealers), money market dealers and funding dealers. The systems can be reconfigured for multiple applications by one dealer and thus adapted for a smaller dealing room environment.

Interbank foreign exchange system

We will look first at the interbank foreign exchange system. Figure 11.1 shows a typical dealer's desk. The spot dealer is in control of a particular currency and takes into his position deals contracted by a separate forward dealer (for a major currency) and by the customer dealers.

The Cititrader foreign exchange system involves a work-station whose processor is a microcomputer, presently an Apple II, housed in the desk of the dealer. Information is entered by an electronic pen which activates a program in the Apple through a graphics or digitising tablet built in the underside of the desk top; the pens work through up to 2 in. of wood. The graphics tablet acts as an advanced keyboard. By placing the pen over a point on the tablet, a co-ordinate is called up which is translated into a letter, digit, word, sentence or calculation which is shown on a screen in front of the dealer. This screen is the

Fig. 11.1   A typical dealer's desk

dealer's electronic blotter: each transaction is recorded and a summary position is reported on the bottom of the screen.

Once the deal has been recorded on the blotter, it is sent to other Apples that compute both the position and the profit, using a weighted average rate. Information is passed through a ribbon of wires to a central machine room and enters an Apple that maintains a deal file; this in turn passes data to other Apples which are managing positions, printing deal tickets, generating broker and other transactional listings, and sending transaction details to the front end of the bank's mainframe computer. The position keeping Apples write information to centralised memory and print a log of every deal that enters the system. The log includes profit and positional information and could be used, if the need arose, to create a new positional record, if for any reason there were a complete system failure. A second safety precaution is the existence of two large Winchester discs, which provide the memory and backup memory to record the positional details.

The position keeping Apples send the positional information they have calculated to a central file that acts as an electronic notice board and displays that information to anyone who is authorised to see it. The positional information contains much more information than the blotter, including cash flow information by month or by day, depending on whether the user is a spot or forward dealer. A spot dealer has his short-date cash flow given to him for the next 31 business days; a forward dealer has monthly information for the next 12 months and a total for flows over 12 months.

The foreign exchange dealers have a standardised tablet overlay that is shown in Fig. 11.2.

The overlay is laid out in such a way that it segregates the various actions taken

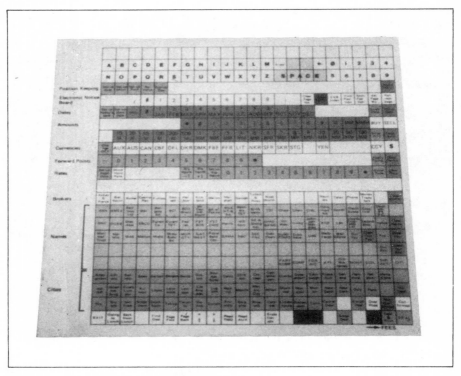

Fig. 11.2   A standardised tablet overlay

to effect a transaction. It is thus possible to enter deal information in any order, without worrying about following a prescribed sequence of inputs.

At the top of the tablet are two rows of letters and numerals which are used to enter free-form names and numbers. The next rows set up the position keeper and the electronic noticeboard, which delivers information from the network to the dealer. The dates row is used to set up the spot rate and provides a simplified entry of other dates. Amounts are input either number by number or by building them up: entering <4MM> followed by <500M> and <50M> puts 4,550,000 on the screen. (The signs, < >, indicate a single press of the pen on the overlay, which enters the information shown on the square that the pen is pressing.) The currency is always against the US dollar and once set up does not need to be changed. The dealer has the facility to switch from one currency to another to enter deals, unless another dealer is managing that currency position. Rates are held at the big figure, so that the dealer has only to enter the two or three digits needed to represent the points. Names are held in two sections, one for brokers and one for counterparties: a single stroke of the pen and the full name of the bank or broker is entered. Unusual names are entered through the alphabet at the top of the screen. Below the names are listed the cities where the counterparties are based. The bottom row is used to manage the tablet once it is working and includes search facilities through the blotter, deal entry and print instructions and system close down.

At the beginning of the day the dealer goes through a simple start-up routine. First he enters the system through his personal password; then he initials the tablet and enters the spot date, the hold rate (used to convert all transactions to a local currency equivalent) and the big figure for the currency (in this case French francs). His blotter now shows his starting position (last night's closing position), which is also his present current position. The dealer completes his start-up routine by now calling up his overnight position, which will be shown to him on the electronic notice board.

To enter a deal, all or part of the following must be put in, in any order: buy/sell amount of currency of US dollars, the rate (defaults to big figure), the date (defaults to spot date), the name, the customer's receive agent, the bank's pay and receive agents (usually provided automatically as a default value by the system), points (for a forward deal) and how the deal was received (from a broker, by telephone or telex).

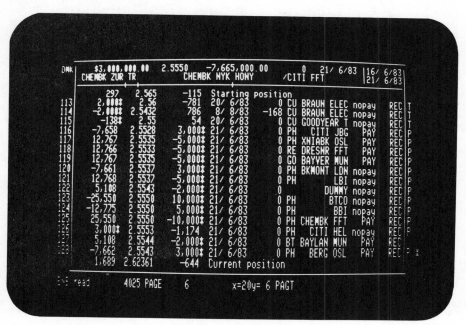

Fig. 11.3   A sample blotter screen

The thin oblong area at the top of the blotter screen shown in Fig. 11.3 is the deal input area and gives the big figure for the currency. Each transaction will be listed below the deal input area every time the dealer authorises a deal. When the screen is full the deals are moved up, so that the last deal done is the deal at the bottom of the page, above the current position. At any time the dealer can look back over his blotter by pressing <page back> or call up a deal into the deal area for enhancement or amendment; strict rules apply to prevent changes being made to details that affect the position and if that is the case a new deal must be entered.

If the dealer is a spot dealer then his position screen will look like the one shown in Fig. 11.4.

```
           DMK SPOT AND SHORT DATE INFORMATION
       DATE 16/ 6/83   SPOT 21/ 6/83     LAST1 TMU
                                         DEAL 129
       ----------------------------------------------
       POSITION                AVE. RATE          2.555
       DMK M            -5975  $M                 2338
       ----------------------------------------------
       SPOT P/L         17296  FWD P/L            5185
       SHORT P/L            0  REBATE            -5548
       TOTAL P/L        16933  NET FWD P/L        -363

       16/ 6    -1225    -1225  5/ 7 -18000 141054
       17/ 6        5    -1220 ■
       20/ 6    26386    25166
       21/ 6   -14475    10691
       22/ 6   -88190   -77498
       23/ 6   -21991   -99489
       24/ 6   -41185  -140674
       27/ 6    74158   -66516
       28/ 6    11765   -54751
       29/ 6   -63126  -117877
       30/ 6    94130   -23747
        1/ 7   182802   159054
```

Fig. 11.4   A spot dealer's position screen

The position screen shown is divided into three areas. At the top are displayed his currency position, the offsetting US dollar position and the average rate of the position. The next area contains profit information: on the left-hand side are the spot and short-date profit/loss that the spot dealer is responsible for. Forward positions are kept on a separate blotter and the profit/loss is reported on the spot position screen on the electronic notice board, together with the value of the last rebate (or revaluation of the forward position) and the total forward profit or loss.

In the bottom part of the screen are shown the cash flows that exist for the short dates, up to 31 days forward. Each entry consists of a date, the cash flow in thousands of currency units and the cumulative cash flow up to that date. Throughout the system a minus sign indicates a short position or cash outflow. At the top right-hand corner of the screen, the deal number shows the last deal entered by the dealer at the time he called up the screen. As this is a notice board the screen will only change when told to do so by the dealer: this requires just a touch of the pen.

A forward position page shows the information by month, with the forward points and the outright rate used to create the US dollar equivalent of the short or long currency position for the month, again shown in thousands of units (see Fig. 11.5).

Let us put in a forward deal. We are the French franc forward dealer at the start of the day, with an overnight short position of just over Ffr 119,000. We

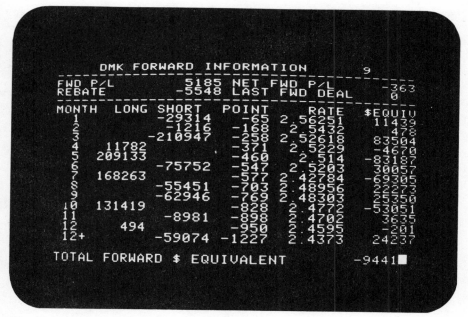

Fig. 11.5   A forward position page

have set up a big figure of 7.09. We now sell over the telephone Ffr 10,000,000 at a spot rate of 7.0855, with 100 forward points and a value date of 23 October 1984, to Chase Manhattan, London, paying the francs to Chase, Paris. The dealer enters, in any order, the information given in Fig. 11.6.

```
(sell) (ccy) (IOMM)...........................the amount
(5) (5) (-) (1) (0) (0) (apply points)...........set up the rate
(enter date) (2) (3) (Oct) (2)..................set up forward date
(phone)......................................how received
(Chase) (London)...............................counterparty
(pay) (Chase) (Paris)..........................delivery
```
Fig. 11.6   Entering dealing information

The system defaults to receive US dollars in the head office in New York and to pay French francs through Citibank in Paris. Only 21 keystrokes were used to create 87 letters or numerals, including the automatic conversion of currency to US dollars. If the dealer is very busy, he needs only to enter the first three lines of data and come back later and enrich the deal with any other information missed. The position will be updated with the basic data. If the dealer is satisfied that the correct information has been entered (corrections are effected by simply overwriting the data), then he presses <deal> which updates his blotter and current position.

If he has all the required fields completed, he can now press <print> which will send the deal to the bank's mainframe computer and will print a deal ticket which may be a mandatory requirement for control purposes, but is not a necessity as far as the system is concerned. The instruction <deal & print> could also be used to combine the two last functions. The system then asks the dealer to confirm the transaction by putting the deal back into the deal area in English and asking the dealer to confirm that 'We sell . . .', to ensure that there is no ambiguity. He now presses <confirm> (or <not confirm> if there is an error) and the deal ticket is printed. The 'P' (meaning deal not yet printed) beside the deal entry on the blotter disappears and the ticket is brought to the dealer for signing.

A swap is entered as a spot deal and a forward outright. However, the second half of the deal is automatically presented to the dealer with the currencies and cash flows reversed, so that he only has to enter the forward date and the swap points to complete the transaction.

A typical deal ticket is shown in Fig. 11.7. Notice that additional information has been added automatically, including the deal number, Fees number (the unique code used to recognise the customer on the book-keeping system), hold rate (the rate used to convert amounts into local currency for book-keeping purposes), the equivalent in local currency (in this case sterling), dealer's initials, boxes for control checks and system references to enable internal checks.

```
              DMKO  SPOT  DEAL

                     NUMBER    124

                     DONE ON  16/ 6/83
                     FEES     001373383


     CUSTOMER              BBI
     FEES A/C NUMBER       865842
     WE BOUGHT             5,000,000.00 DOLLARS
     WE SOLD               12,775,000.00 DMK
     AT                    2.5550
     FORWARD POINTS                  0.00
     BOUGHT RATE           1.52
     SOLD RATE             3.8836
     STERLING EQUIVALENT   3,289,473.68
     HOLD RATE             1.52
     VALUE                 21/ 6/83
     BROKEN                PH

     OUR RECEIVE AGENT     HONY

     THEIR RECEIVE AGENT   nopaw

     OUR PAY AGENT         CITI FFT

     DEAL DONE BY          KRB

                                                          The attached
                                                          dealing telex has
     Dealer        Stage1            Stage2      Verify   been checked by :
   ---------------------------------------------------------------------------
   |            |                 |            |        |                    |
   |            |  Automatic      |            |        |                    |
   |            |  Transmission   |            |        |                    |
   |            |     to          |            |        |                    |
   |            |   FEES          |            |        |                    |
   ---------------------------------------------------------------------------

              [Ticket serial no 10118]
```

Fig. 11.7   A typical deal ticket

Each time the system is used, a log is made of that usage. The system generates various other listings and deal logs. One important listing is a brokers' list, which shows each deal done and sorted by the broker. This enables checks with brokers that transactions can be confirmed quickly and effectively. Automation of this simple task saves an unexpected amount of time.

Transactions can be routed through the network to be reported on the position of the dealer concerned. Thus, the customer transactions, which are contracted in a separate dealing room, are delivered electronically to the two or more dealers involved. Both the format of the overlay and the display on the VDU can be changed to meet the requirements of groups of dealers, and in a limited way, those of individual dealers.

Money market dealer's system

On the face of it, the money market dealers have a completely different system, which is based on a similar approach to deal input and which generates asset and liability management information. Their overlay is laid out differently to reflect the functions of the normal transactions carried out by the funding managers. The layout of the overlay can be seen to be quite flexible, as is the format of the screen (see Fig. 11.8).

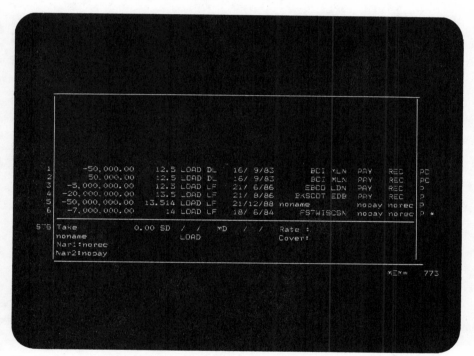

Fig. 11.8   A money market dealer's screen

The deal entry is now in the lower box with the blotter above it. All fixed-rate loans and deposits are entered into the system and the input and recall of deals is similar to the foreign exchange systems. Data can be displayed by overwriting the blotter area with various pages of information, such as daily and monthly projections of transactions entered into the system. The most important information displays are the asset and liability screens. These show the volumes and average rates of assets and liabilities for each period, the resulting gaps, the profit or loss associated with those gaps, the cost of closing the gaps at today's rates and the rates themselves used in the calculations. The system permits sensitivity analyses to be carried out on the rate data to show the impact of changes in overall rates or the yield curve on the existing or projected earnings. A sample short-term screen is shown in Fig. 11.9 which gives monthly positions; longer-term screens are also available.

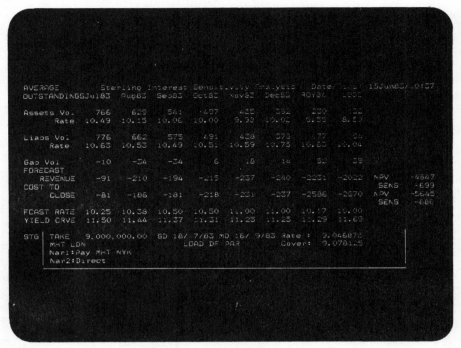

Fig. 11.9   A short-term asset and liability screen

As with the foreign exchange dealer, the money market dealer has on-line information which concerns his interest rate book and he can see the impact of each transaction on his overall position as the transaction is booked. He can see instantly the risk associated with his position and the cost to close shows the value of the position at this point in time, which may differ significantly from the revenue expected if the interest rates were predicted to move in the dealer's favour.

Each system is designed to speed up deal entry and as a result present information quickly to the main users, the dealers. In addition, management can have access to the system and call up the various screens on the electronic notice board. Data in the system can also be used to create management information.

A separate touch sensitive pad is used by the treasurer and the chief dealer either to call up screens or to review the transactions performed by an individual dealer. The pad activates a special program which reads the deal file and graphically presents the deal information (see Fig. 11.10). This enables deals booked at rates outside the day's 'norm' to be inspected. By moving the pointer at the top of the screen over the deal to be investigated, the graph is replaced by a screen which shows summary details of the transaction in question, including the initials of the dealer who authorised the deal.

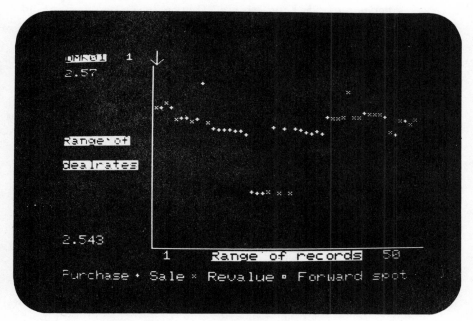

Fig. 11.10   Graphic representation of deal information

Other applications of the system

Cititrader was an early and very successful application of networked microcomputers. It is a measure of the growth of the financial markets that the computers used in the development of the network are now too small and the system is being enhanced by Citibank to include, among other things, the range of dealers' aids offered by other front-end systems. This will require other, more powerful, microcomputers. The product is available commercially on a network using IBM-PCs; a stand-alone PC version is also available.

The stand-alone IBM-PC provides all the functions of a networked system and shows the difference in power between an eight-bit and a 16-bit system, as it can handle the work that two Apple IIs are needed for. The PC manages the graphics tablet input and up to two printers, one for logging all transactions that go across the position, the other for printing deal tickets. The system has been successfully installed in banks in London, which are using them to gain experience of this unique method of capturing data. Several banks are specifying networked-based IBM-PC systems and the basic Cititrader software will be changed to meet their special requirements.

The Cititrader approach is important for several reasons. It uses small computers in combinations that achieve considerable data processing capability, with on-line delivery of essential information for the user. The method of entering data through a digitising tablet could be used for any application. The speed at which it was developed and introduced shows the flexibility of micro-computers. The cost was sufficiently low for the Citibank treasury to be able to develop and install its own system in parallel with the bank's book-keeping systems. Elements of this approach are likely to be incorporated in other treasury management software packages in the future.

Possible applications to the treasury function

The dealing system has solved one of the fundamental problems of data management, the early capture of information, which removes the need to re-enter that data for processing on separate computer systems. It is not intended to replace back-office systems, but it does offer a way to make the whole process more productive and streamlined. In a bank, the treasury operation can stand almost completely in isolation from the other activities of the bank, as long as it can feed the transactional details into the mainframe to keep customer accounts up-to-date. This independence can be seen in treasury functions in other types of companies, and where access to information is needed quickly or when creation of information is labour-intensive, the solution offered by the dealing system described above may be worth considering.

Treasury management organisation

Each major bank has its own philosophy with regard to the way it organises its treasury departments. Chase's investment in its new dealing room represents the bank's individual approach to this business, as does Citibank's investment in small computers. Other banks have different problems and priorities and each bank learns from the successes of others. The investment in treasury systems, in new dealing rooms and improved communications equipment is only a small part of the investment that most banks are making in technology.

Treasury management is being recognised in Europe as an important component in the success of any company, not just of banks. In many cases money management is a self-contained world which makes little impact on the day-to-day commercial business of the company, yet its timely intervention can greatly improve profit performance. At a mundane level, control of cash movements is a critical factor in evaluating the effectiveness of a company's financial discipline; in managerial terms, a lack of discipline can be seen in companies that suffer unexpected losses caused by the massive swings in exchange rates between one year and the next. Companies that manage this problem effectively are still rare in the UK, although the problem is a topic of major study and concern in the US.

As European companies develop their treasury operations they will find little help in looking at the way banks organise their treasuries, except in the areas of operational expertise. Banks tend to be outstanding in terms of transactional processing. As companies centralise certain treasury operations into clearing or re-invoicing centres, they will need to develop efficient transaction processing systems of their own. The advent of large capacity micro-computers means that banks can easily transfer part of their expertise in operations management to their customers.

Part Three

The electronic treasurer

CHAPTER 12

Electronics in the treasury

The use of computers and telecommunications equipment requires a technical specialist. Close involvement in the financial markets requires an equally specialised person. Most corporations do not have the second-by-second involvement of banks to justify the employment of specialised dealers and operations staff. Neither can they afford to invest in the development of computer and communications systems used by banks to manage their activities. However, banks are now making available their data bases and computer systems through electronic banking systems. Microcomputers allow even small companies to buy in or develop their own treasury management systems cheaply.

We now return to the corporate treasurer and look at the way that the environment is changing around him. Let us look first at how he can use one of the basic tools, a microcomputer, to help him in his day-to-day work and then look at the more complex computer systems available to him.

Uses of microcomputers

In the first chapter of this book we looked at a treasurer of a trading company and how he went about raising working capital. In the example given he looked at the markets and consulted with the customer dealer at his bank. Between them they agreed to use the cheaper of dollar or sterling bankers' acceptances to fund the company's need for sterling working capital. The dealer then obtained the rates needed to compare the cost of the instruments. You will recall that to calculate the comparative costs the following considerations are important.

1.   Bankers' acceptances are quoted at a discounted rate and these rates will have to be converted to a true yield to compare them to LIBO rates.
2.   Calculation of yields must therefore take into account the lost opportunity of paying interest at the front-end for the bankers' acceptances.
3.   Sterling is quoted on a 365-day basis and US dollars on a 360-day basis.
4.   Spreads, that is, the bank's margin, will be different for the different instruments.

Let us see how we can use a microcomputer to help decide the best way to finance this requirement. The most obvious application for a microcomputer is to perform the myriad calculations needed in the day-to-day management of financial problems. Its superiority over programmable calculators is most apparent in terms of ease of use and storage of information over periods of time. Half-way between a programmable calculator and a specially written piece of applications software are spreadsheet utilities, such as Visicalc, which share some of the software program's superior features, but are not as user friendly when it comes to complex problems that have to be solved by several different people who may not be familiar with the software. Presentation of information is also less attractive. Rather than provide an exhaustive list of the various calculations that can be carried out in the search for the best profit opportunity at any time, it is probably more productive to look at one particular type of transaction and see how to apply the new electronic technology to it.

A sample transaction

The formula to calculate the effective, all-in rate becomes even more complex when the foreign exchange aspects are included. Let us assume we need some US dollar financing and we want to check the rate that we can obtain by funding the loan with sterling bankers' acceptances and swapping into dollars. To eliminate foreign exchange risk we need to buy back our sterling at the forward date with the US dollars we are receiving on the forward date. The discount rate we have been offered for our sterling must be converted to a true yield, using the formula given below.

$$\text{True yield} = \text{Discount rate} \div \frac{(1 - (\text{Discount rate} \times \text{Days to maturity}))}{36,500}$$

Our US dollar equivalent rate is derived from the swap cost, adjusted for the different number of days in the year, and is equivalent to:

$$\frac{\left\{\left[\left(\dfrac{\text{Yield}}{100} \times \dfrac{\text{Days}}{365}\right) + 1\right] \times \left[\left(\text{Spot rate} + \dfrac{\text{Forward points}}{10,000}\right) - \text{Spot rate}\right]\right\} \times 36,000}{\text{Days} \times \text{Spot rate}}$$

In the formula 'days' stands for days to maturity.

Let us put this on to a spreadsheet program (see Fig. 12.1). We will be collecting the variables on rows 10 to 13, showing the yield on row 17 and the US dollar rate on row 19.

The formula in F19 is shown at the top of the screen as the cursor is resting on that cell at the present time. The formula can easily be copied in other cells and if we moved to the left, to E19, we would see the same formula, but with the references changed to cells in column E. Thus we can enter data in E10 to E13 or P10 to P13 and get answers calculated on the same basis in cells E19 and P19.

We would have to collect some more data and create another similar calculation to get comparable information on generating sterling from dollar instruments. Using the Lotus spreadsheet, we could store the information and

```
                                                              READY
F19:(((((F17/100)*F11/365))+1)*(F12+(F13/10000))-F12)*36000)/F11*F12)

        A         B         C         D         E         F         G
   4
   5
   6
   7
   8
   9
  10             sterling interest rate            12         9      11.75
  11             number of days                    30        30        30
  12             dollar/sterling spot rate       2.07       1.5       1.5
  13             forward points                   150         7         7
  14
  15
  16
  17             true yield                   12.11953  9.067071  11.86458
  18
  19             US dollar rate               20.73578  9.507038  12.26751
  20
  21
  22
  23
```

Fig. 12.1   A sample spreadsheet program

put the data on a graph to show the differences in funding costs over time. So why bother with a long program if spreadsheets are so easy and so versatile? The only reason is that the program can be more user friendly, as it can have logic traps to reject faulty input and it takes the user through the program, an important factor if the user does not use the program very often. The spreadsheet is, however, more than adequate for the needs of most managers once they have found their way about the software.

A sample program

The program that is shown in the Appendix compares the financing costs of dollar and sterling bankers' acceptances, using the money market rates and foreign exchange rates to look for the most attractive way to borrow money to finance trade-related transactions. The calculation needs to take into account the several considerations outlined on page 105.

Our program is functional rather than elegant. It was written quickly by two dealers in London to solve an urgent need in their dealing room and has been in daily use for a number of years. This version has been tidied up to run on an IBM-PC. The output from the original program is circulated by the dealers in hard copy and over a network of video terminals to show other parts of the bank the relative values of the financing alternatives available. When the program starts up, the first screen is a simple reminder to check that the printer is on.

Once the user has started up the program he sees the screen given in Fig. 12.2. It is divided into four areas and the user will enter data into the top and left-hand areas: the program will calculate and fill the right-hand and bottom parts of the screen.

The program takes its 'today's' date from the current date entered into the computer as part of its start-up routine. The value date is the first business day after today or defaults to today's date. Spot is the current US dollar/sterling exchange rate. The final piece of information needed is the RAC, the sterling reserve asset cost that the bank involved has to pay for making loan fixtures. A

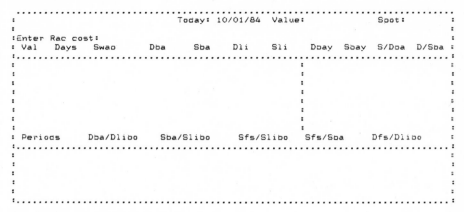

```
:..........................................................................:
:                               Today: 10/01/84  Value:          Spot:    :
:                                                                          :
:Enter Rac cost:                                                           :
: Val   Days  Swap      Dba     Sba     Dli     Sli     Dpay  Spay  S/Dpa  D/Spa :
:..........................................................................:
:                                                            :             :
:                                                            :             :
:                                                            :             :
:                                                            :             :
:                                                            :             :
:                                                            :             :
: Periods      Dba/Dlibo     Sba/Slibo     Sfs/Slibo   Sfs/Spa     Dfs/Dlibo   :
:..........................................................................:
:                                                                          :
:                                                                          :
:                                                                          :
:                                                                          :
:                                                                          :
:..........................................................................:
```

Fig. 12.2   Preliminary screen

feature of the program is some effective, if somewhat rudimentary, error trapping. Thus, incorrect dates would be rejected and the operator asked to re-enter them. The screen is reproduced in Fig. 12.3 showing data entered for the four periods that the bank will accept.

```
:..........................................................................:
: Press <C> to calc:              Today: 10/01/84  Value: 11/01/84  Spot: 1.3490 :
:       (Rac: .08)                                                         :
: Val   Days  Swap      Dba     Sba     Dli     Sli     Dpay  Spay  S/Dpa  D/Spa :
:..........................................................................:
: 10/02  30    3     5     9.50    9.03    9.75    9.45 :                   :
:                                                      :                   :
: 12/03  61   10    14     9.45    8.98    9.88    9.52 :                   :
:                                                      :                   :
: 10/04  90   16    19     9.45    8.92   10.00    9.58 :                   :
:                                                      :                   :
: 10/07 181   34    38     9.45    9.16   10.19    9.83 :                   :
:                                                      :                   :
: Periods      Dba/Dlibo     Sba/Slibo     Sfs/Slibo   Sfs/Spa     Dfs/Dlibo   :
:..........................................................................:
:                                                                          :
:                                                                          :
:                                                                          :
:                                                                          :
:                                                                          :
:..........................................................................:
```

Fig. 12.3   Second screen

Once up to four periods have been entered, the user presses <C> and is presented with the results of the computations as shown in Fig. 12.4.

By pressing <P> the headings are explained as in Fig. 12.5.

<SHIFT–PrtSc> is used to print out the contents of the screen ('PrtSc' is a special function key on the IBM-PC). The program can easily be extended to store data and recall them at a later date.

A word of caution: the program looks complex and may be more complex than it needs to be, but once the originators move on it may be difficult to change or add to it. Where programs become essential to day-to-day activities they must be fully documented, with full indices of variables used. If it takes several pages of code to manage a relatively simple problem, consider how many volumes of code will be needed to solve a problem twice as large. Most of the code will be inefficient, but will you have the energy (or can you afford the luxury) to go back and make the program shorter and more effective? If the program works securely then elegance is a function of professional pride rather than necessity.

```
:...........................................................................:
:                             Today: 10/01/84  Value: 11/01/84  Spot: 1.3490  :
:      (Rac: .08)                                                             :
:  Val  Days   Swap     Dba     Sba     Dli    Sli    Dbay  Sbay  S/Dba  D/Sba :
:...........................................................................:
: 10/02  30    3     5   9.50    9.03    9.75   9.45 :  9.58  9.10  9.44   9.41 :
:                                                    :                         :
: 12/03  61   10    14   9.45    8.98    9.88   9.52 :  9.60  9.12  9.30   9.59 :
:                                                    :                         :
: 10/04  90   16    19   9.45    8.92   10.00   9.58 :  9.68  9.12  9.34   9.55 :
:                                                    :                         :
: 10/07 181   34    38   9.45    9.16   10.19   9.83 :  9.92  9.60  9.54  10.03 :
:                                                                             :
: Periods      Dba/Dlibo     Sba/Slibo      Sfs/Slibo    Sfs/Sba     Dfs/Dlibo :
:...........................................................................:
:   30          0.17          0.35           0.01        -0.35        0.34     :
:                                                                             :
:   61          0.28          0.40           0.22        -0.18        0.29     :
:                                                                             :
:   90          0.32          0.46           0.24        -0.22        0.45     :
:                                                                             :
:  181          0.27          0.23           0.29         0.05        0.16     :
:...........................................................................:
  Waiting for (SHIFT-PrtSc) or (P)
```

Fig. 12.4   Results of the computations

```
*** KEY ***

Dba/Dlibo ... dollar libo minus dollar ba yield

Sba/Slibo ... stg libo minus stg ba yield

Sfs/Slibo ... stg libo minus fully swapped stg from dollar ba

Sfs/Sba   ... stg ba minus fully swapped stg from dollar ba

Dfs/Dlibo ... dollar libo minus fully swapped dollars from sterling ba

Dbay and Sbay are dollar and sterling ba yields

D/sba and S/dba are dollar and sterling costs
fully swapped from sterling and dollar ba's
```

Fig. 12.5   Explanation of headings

Uses of dealers' aids

In a busy dealing room it has proved preferable to have dedicated programs rather than to use spreadsheet applications. However, spreadsheets are invaluable in developing the logic that is needed to make the programs work. The inventory of dealers' aids gets longer and longer and includes programs to calculate ECUs and SDRs, cross rates and break-even rates for financial futures. Wherever possible a dealers' aid prints out the deal tickets that result from transactions which may arise from quoting rates created by the program. The most sophisticated dealers' aid, a networked position keeping system, is described in Chapter 13.

Dealer's aids should also be used by company treasurers to give an indication as to how the market is going and the level of rates to expect from the banks. Treasurers of companies have their own problems and some of these are well suited to the sort of small program used in our rate comparison program. One problem is simply to work out what to do.

To give an example, suppose we know that we have Deutschmark income in a few months' time. How should we cover the foreign exchange exposure? Should we cover forward or should we borrow the Deutschmarks, convert them into sterling and invest them, letting the future inflow settle the debt? Either way is effective and theoretically both should yield the same result, but if the markets are out of line then one method would be cheaper than the other. The calculation is not completely straightforward, but depends on how interest has to be treated. The calculation is sufficiently tedious to stop people performing it as a matter of course. Once on a computer, the information can be derived easily at any time by just putting in the constituent parts of the equation.

Many companies have a problem in that they have a large number of banking and borrowing facilities, each subtly different. Each one has a different rate structure – base rate for overdrafts, LIBOR for fixtures, discount rates for acceptances – as well as different spreads, fees and commissions. Some of these facilities will be used fully, some hardly at all. Assuming that the basic market rates will be the same from each bank, the treasurer will want to use the cheapest facility first. A program to calculate availability under credit lines and the add-on cost of using the line also provides a diary system that can be used to keep track of facilities and with a little extra programming could generate confirmation letters and internal accounting media.

Virtually every office job can be streamlined and enhanced by using microcomputers; the slowness to capitalise on these new tools is partly due to deeply ingrained beliefs that computers are expensive and difficult to program. The above are just a few examples as to how they can be used.

Charting

One important use of electronics is in presenting information through services such as Reuters and taking that information and using it for analysis of past and present events. Forecasting of interest and foreign exchange rates has always been difficult and the volatility of the markets in the last few years has made traditional methods, based on economic fundamentals that no longer seem to apply, even more unreliable. The increasing volumes of business now being channelled through the financial futures markets in the US have brought considerable focus on charting and the computer systems that can be used to obtain the charts needed for forecasting.

Charting is a stock market and commodity trading technique that attempts to look for mathematical relationships between the movements of rates and to predict the future accordingly. What is needed is a data base and the exhaustive testing of mathematical formulae to create a relationship between the movement of the rates and future expectations. Sooner or later human judgement has to be brought into the equation, making the resulting forecast just as dubious as those produced by other methods.

The creation of raw charts by a computer is relatively simple. Data are fed in by a telephone link from a data base and a program generates the chart from the data. In the US, the charts are themselves provided over the telephone. The most useful mathematical analyses are comparisons of moving averages of varying length and the fitting of momentum curves to measure the amount of change in the movement of the rates that are under scrutiny.

Financial charts are delivered electronically by several systems in the UK, including the stock market charts provided by Datastream. In the exchange and money markets two very similar systems are available that chart rates move-by-move as they are reported, with the output available for display instantly, either on screens or as printed hard copy of the screens. Needless to say, these services are expensive, but are important to market participants, such as brokers, who attract their clients by their ability to provide up-to-the minute information.

Conceptually, charting has little to distinguish it from any other form of divining or soothsaying; its importance is due to the fact that so many people, particularly in the US, follow the charts religiously. Serious market users need to know when the charts will indicate a significant movement in the market, which can happen when certain pre-ordained points on a trend line have been reached.

Management uses of electronic banking

If we return to our example of the trading company treasurer, let us assume that he has now placed his business with his bank. He has borrowed US dollars and has swapped them into sterling to fund his working capital needs. In fact he will not need the funds for a few days, so that he will be investing the sterling as soon as it becomes available. On the forward date he will receive US dollars which he will use to liquidate his forward foreign exchange deal.

Money is flowing in and out of accounts and the treasurer will use his electronic banking terminal to keep track of what is going on. The treasurer's interests go beyond his immediate concern for the parent or holding company for which he works. He is also concerned with the financial activities of the domestic and overseas subsidiaries that the company owns. These may or may not report to the treasurer, but he has a management brief to ensure that the cash management of the total corporation is properly managed and that banking arrangements are both logical and efficient.

Before he got his electronic banking terminal the treasurer or his assistant would have had to call the subsidiaries of the parent company or their banks around the world to get information on particular accounts or wait to receive a telex to give him the same information. This is still an adequate means of getting information if activity is quite light. In Japan, balance and basic statement information can be obtained by using a very small device that fits over the mouthpiece of a telephone, and by using numerical codes bleeped through the telephone by the device, a speaking computer is activated at the bank. The computer voice gives out details as required in a rather American accent, but it certainly achieves its purpose. Electronic banking enables the treasurer to get information at any time of the day, even when the account is in a bank overseas which is closed due to holiday or time differences.

Electronic banking provides access to all this information by tapping into the data highways set up by the international banks, initially for their own use, latterly for the use of their customers. The larger banks have elaborate communications systems of their own, with satellites and telephone networks that join up virtually every part of the globe. Banks have realised that their business is just as much about information, its processing and its distribution, as it is about lending money.

Sitting in his office in London, the treasurer can see how his subsidiaries are using the various facilities available from each bank that provides an electronic banking service. He can see the balances on accounts in West Germany and Hong Kong, get transactional details of particular entries, see how long loans have been drawn down, check the usage of foreign exchange or forecast the cash outflows and inflows over the next few days.

Each bank will try to get him to take their own terminal in his office. After a short time the treasurer should be able to evaluate those services that truly help him and those that do not. If he has a wide range of banks he will want to reduce unnecessary clutter and adapt a single terminal, probably a microcomputer such as an IBM-PC, which will accept information from any bank.

The treasurer's office is becoming an electronic playground, with banking terminals, Reuters and Telerate monitors, charting services, special applications run on microcomputers and terminals which connect with the company's mainframe and electronic mail services. In this part of the book we will look at some of the electronic banking facilities available to the treasurer. We start by looking at the impact electronics have made on all forms of banking, because it is important to bear in mind that some of the new techniques in handling personal business could find applications in the way banking services are provided for corporate clients. We then move on to look at specific electronic banking services.

CHAPTER 13

Technological changes in banking

'Electronic banking' means different things to different people. To the High Street banker it conjures up visions of rows of cash dispensing machines standing in gleaming replacement of bank staff and reducing the need to speak to that most difficult of visitors, the paying customer. To the commercial banker it means a terminal in every customer's office, bringing together the customer's computer and that of the bank whenever possible and placing the onus of accuracy squarely on the shoulders of the customer. The customer has the benefits of convenience of execution of transactions and access to more information then ever before (and the underlying assumption on both sides is that he wants them).

Technology has made dramatic changes to the way that banking services are delivered and effected. These changes are more obvious in the way that we use banks as individuals, as customers in the retail banking market. Changes in the services provided for corporations in the commercial banking market are equally significant. In this chapter we will look first at the way that retail banking is changing and then at the more general aspects of change in the banking system that will affect the corporate treasurer directly.

Effects on retail banking services

Automated tellers

The use of electronics in retail banking has seen the widespread introduction of automated bank tellers that now provide an impressive range of services (in addition to dispensing cash), including reporting of bank balances and transfer of funds from one account to another. Many bank customers prefer to use automated tellers rather than queuing up and confronting the real thing.

Automated tellers have an added advantage in that they can be located close to the customer, either where he works or where he spends his money. For example, all four clearing banks have installed cash machines in the new food store opened by Sainsbury's at Crystal Palace.

The plastic card that is used to activate the machine has a magnetic strip on which is encoded the secret identification password that the customer must enter through the teller's keyboard; the password on the card is compared with the password entered and if it does not match up on the second or third attempt then the machine confiscates the card. The automated tellers are micro-computers that are connected to the bank's local mainframe which controls the availability of cash withdrawal, against either credit balances or credit limits.

Heavy investment in electronics is a means of raising barriers to entry into the banks' traditional preserves, while the increased efficiency will hopefully woo customers away from other types of financial institutions. In most countries banks do not have the lion's share of the retail market, but fall behind the savings industry in the competition for the individual customer's business. The aggressiveness of the banking system in part depends on its ability to compete on the same terms as the savings companies, which often enjoy special privileges or government protection. The banking system's success or failure depends on its effectiveness in capturing the salary payments of the working population. Surprisingly, in most countries cash or cheques are still the normal means of payment; the UK, with its legendary armies of 'unbanked' working people, has the highest proportion of direct credit transfer of salaries, when compared with other industrialised nations.

It is the continuing importance of cash and cheques that is causing the clearing banks to embrace the use of automated tellers so enthusiastically. In the UK, over 90 per cent of all transactions are still settled in cash, 15 per cent of all adults deal only in cash and 40 per cent of all adults never go into a bank, but keep their money with institutions such as building societies. Forty-four per cent of all working adults still get paid in cash and resist fiercely any suggestion of change. Around 40 per cent of bank staff spend their whole time handling cash and cheque payments and the proportion of staff handling these types of transactions is similar in a savings institution and much higher in a credit or charge card company.

Automated tellers are an important way for banks to differentiate them-selves from each other, but they face competition from the credit and charge card companies, particularly Visa. Visa is a credit card company that is owned by its members, which are the banks that issue the card (for example, Barclays in the UK). Visa is now setting up cash dispensers with the intention of providing the user with cash from his account anywhere in the world. Visa intends to place these machines in airports and railway stations, as well as in any branch of its 15,000 members who will take them; there is some disquiet among those members who see the use of a universal system as a threat to their customer base.

The UK banks, however, seem confident that product differentiation can be maintained even if the customers of different financial institutions use the same terminals. Thus, the customers of the National Westminster and Midland Banks can use the terminals of either bank with the card issued to them by their own bank. Lloyds, Barclays and the Royal Bank of Scotland have a similar arrangement. Both networks have around 1,700 machines, some inside the banks themselves, some in remote locations.

Experiments to take machine-based banking even further are being tried out. The National Westminster in Basingstoke has divided its banking hall in two. One area is for conventional banking and the other is for machine-based banking, with different types of automated tellers that take deposits as well as dispense cash, a safe deposit machine with special computerised cash and cheque counting facilities and booths containing computers connected to the branch computer which allow the customer to obtain detailed information on his account and on individual transactions, with hard copy printed off if so required. The automated part opens earlier and closes later than the conventional part of the banking hall.

The use of automated tellers makes the distinction between the services offered by building societies and clearing banks even more blurred. As building societies continue aggressively to expand their branch networks, they are meeting the same cost constraints that are forcing the banks into electronic-based services. Some, particularly the Halifax, are setting up automated teller networks of their own. Others are joining together with the clearers to provide access for their customers to the clearing banks' network of automated teller machines. Nationwide, with its arrangement with Barclays, is a good case in point.

Home banking

Indeed, the first real attempt to provide home banking services in the UK has come from the initiative of the Nottingham Building Society, which has joined with the Bank of Scotland to provide a Prestel-based facility. The Bank of Scotland provides a cheque book, a Visa card that works on the Barclays cash machines and cash withdrawal facilities at branches of Thomas Cook. Over a Prestel link, with the connecting adaptor provided free to customers with mortgages or balances over £10,000, the subscriber can call up his bank or building society accounts, make certain types of payments, view the electronic catalogues of shops and estate and travel agents, apply for loans and write letters to the two financial sponsors of the scheme.

Home banking has been made possible by the development in West Germany of gateway technology, whereby the viewdata computer can interrogate large data bases in banks or other institutions and therefore does not have to manage massive data bases of its own. This type of technology is widely used in West Germany and Scandinavia (where home banking is more extensively available) and in the US, where Chemical Bank's Pronto and competing services use the same approach. The cost of the service also therefore includes the cost of being connected to Prestel, which makes a charge each time the system is accessed.

Effects of competition

Another major factor in the increasing use of electronic banking is de-regulation, which exposes banks to the competition, while making the consumer more aware of better ways of investing or borrowing his money. In the US, where overdrafts are virtually unknown, the move to casual credit has been followed by the explosive growth of credit cards. In Europe, the banks in some countries, notably West Germany, have protected themselves by restricting their own marketing of credit cards, while providing automatic overdraft facilities related to the customer's income stream. The freer availability of credit makes the individual less concerned with liquidity and the need to keep the bank manager happy in case he is needed to help out on a rainy day. Savings per capita are rising steadily throughout most of the world and here, too, the consumer is becoming more sophisticated, as the massive swings of savings in the US, first from low-yielding bank passbooks into high-yielding money fund accounts and then into the banks' competitive super NOW accounts, have shown.

Easy movement of funds is an important factor that the electronic age has brought to the competition between financial institutions. Automated tellers, home banking and point of sale funds transfers, when added to the increasing useof standing orders and direct debits, have a major benefit in addition to reducing paper flows. The customer now keys the transaction, when he makes a request for funds movement, into the automated teller or, in the future, into his home banking terminal. Bank branches will be used more and more as financial supermarkets, providing services such as estate agency, insurance broking, travel and tax planning. This helps explain the still significant growth of bank andbuilding society branches throughout the UK, which is not usual among other European countries at a time when heavy investment in automated tellers is still under way.

Credit and charge cards

Electronics are now stretching out to transform the credit and charge card industries by connecting the retailer directly to the card company. Every shop or restaurant has a limit and it checks with the credit card company for any amount over that limit to ensure that the customer is within his credit agreement. This is done over the telephone and the process is speeded up by a modem that automatically connects with the card company and reads the credit card number to the computer, so that the account details are in front of the authoriser by the time approval is requested.

Reducing the flows of paper, caused either by cheque- or credit-card-based transactions, is the prime motive behind other experiments. In France, credit cards are being tested that have chips built into the magnetic strip which hold details of the customer's credit line and of the amount remaining unused. The cash register reads the information on the chip and if a purchase is made, reduces the amount available for the card for future transactions. When the account is settled with the bank, the bank restores the credit line on the chip to the original position.

In the UK, trials are under way of petrol pumps which automatically read charge cards to pay for petrol without the need for human intervention. Amoco and Barclays have a scheme whereby the motorist uses a card and a coded password to pay for the petrol and the processor in the pump approves the payment once it has checked the information on the card, the password and the credit standing of the card holder. At the end of the day the bank's computer checks with the machine in the pump, gathers details of the transactions that have been carried out, and bills the motorists' accounts accordingly. Petrol payments account for over one-third of all credit card transactions and removal of the related paper flow will make both garages and credit card companies more efficient.

Banks do not like credit cards, with their implications of float-free credit until settlement being offered to the consumer, and given the choice, the banks would prefer to replace them with debit cards that immediately make a charge to a bank account each time a transaction takes place. In France, another trial has been started to test a system that enables the shopper to make a payment by authorising with a private password the sum needed to settle the bill; this sum is automatically charged to the bank account, although the banks involved have had to introduce an artificial delay of three days between receiving the instruction and settlement to keep their customers happy. Neither of the French test markets has aroused great public interest and they are more important in the evaluation of the technology (which appears to have performed well) than in understanding the consumers' reaction. However much the banks may want them, debit cards are not likely to be introduced in the UK in the near future, as the banks will take a long time to agree standards that will allow this sort of development. Consumers, used to getting several days' free credit with cheques and around a month's free credit with a card, are unlikely to welcome a development of this sort.

EFTPOS

EFTPOS – 'electronic funds transfer from the point of sale' – is unlikely to catch on unless the banking system pays for the hardware. It does, however, demonstrate how microprocessors elevate even the most ordinary machines to new levels of prominence. For years the biggest preoccupation of cash till manufacturers was making efficient motors to open and shut the tills, which often have to hold half a hundred-weight or more of coins and notes. The modern shop tills, in addition to their adaptation to read bar codes for pricing and stock control, can now be used to effect EFTPOS transactions and are becoming the key piece of equipment in many retail businesses.

Electronic funds transfer

The use of automated techniques in the provision of retail banking services is the tip of an iceberg of computerisation that all banks have had to undertake to keep up with the flows of paper created by their transactions. Most of this investment is in automating the back office processes and the book-keeping requirements. However, there are also significant changes in an area that concerns treasurers, electronic funds transfer. The movement of funds between one bank and another, sometimes across national boundaries, creates an enormous number of transactions every day which have to be laboriously fulfilled, recorded and reconciled. All of these activities are being computerised and automated.

There are two main areas of funds transfer, within the local currency, and between different countries or currencies.

Local funds transfer

In the US the funds transfer system is complicated by the interaction between the various federal and state regulations. The payments of large amounts is settled by using the automated Fed wire service or through correspondent banks. Banks using the Fed wire settle their payments through their account with their regional federal reserve bank, which credits the account of the counterparty at his regional Fed. The bank wire is a separate system that is used to advise payments made through either the Fed wire or correspondent banks. The Fed also runs cheque processing and clearings, but the major clearing is that of the independent New York Clearing House and of its Clearing House Interbank Payment System, or CHIPS. CHIPS has a central computer that links up with its membership of about 100 banks. Payments in and out flow through the Reserve Bank of New York on a same-day value basis. All these services are heavily computerised.

Money payments in the UK are not automated to anything like the same extent. However, if New York has its CHIPS, London has its appropriately named CHAPS, the Clearing House Automated Payments System. In London, payments are settled through two clearings, the town clearing and the general clearing. A small dollar clearing also exists. Cheques for the town clearing must be for at least £10,000 and be drawn on a town branch of a clearing bank. CHAPS will replace the town clearing.

The London general clearing is an antique happening in terms of modern technology, with pieces of paper, cheques and payment orders brought by hand into a central hall where they are sorted and delivered to the tables of the clearing banks, which then settle with the Bank of England. The town clearing, while accounting for less than 1 per cent of the number of transactions, manages over 90 per cent of the value of funds moved, as these are mainly the interbank settlements arising out of foreign exchange and money market deals. These payments are 'walked' around the City, so that debit and credit entries can be passed before the end of that day's business. Town cheques receive same-day value, while other cheques take about three days to clear. Payments may also be made by using BACS, the Bankers Automatic Clearing System, which handles electronically standardised payment instructions delivered in the form of computer tape. BACS, which is owned by the major British banks, is a well automated process, with companies delivering payment instructions on computer tapes or similar storage media or by passing instructions directly over British Telecom's packet switching network. The BACS computers pass the necessary entries over the bank accounts concerned. The system is used for making large numbers of regular payments, such as salaries, and is gaining popularity for making direct debits to settle transactions such as insurance premiums.

CHAPS was behind schedule with regard to implementation, but was successfully launched in the first half of 1984. The change that will be most noticeable will be the reduction in the numbers of messengers who throng the streets of the City of London most of the working day. With regard to funds transfer, the system will extend the ability to make same-day value payments, information concerning receipts of funds will be speeded up and settlement between banks and the Bank of England effected electronically. The computers of the settlement banks are connected through telephone lines to the participants' offices. Payments entered by the participant are channelled through the settlement banks and automatically reported to the recipient.

Settlement banks are able to place limits on participants that use CHAPS, as once a payment is entered it will be guaranteed. CHAPS will make the town clearing accessible to all banks in the UK and will reduce some of the special advantages presently enjoyed by the clearers.

CHAPS is a very secure system, more so than its counterparts in the US. Once authorised, payments will be made without any conditions attached and will not be able to be recalled. There is no central computer, but a system of gateways linking the participants feeds payment messages into British Telecom's packet switching service. The banks need only have compatible communications software and are free to provide any additional services to their customers, based on the CHAPS facilities, and to charge for services as they see fit. The settlement banks have between them invested some £8 million in new computers to provide the gateway technology needed.

International funds transfer

Compared with moving money about in one country, moving money internationally is less complex superficially, but this apparent simplicity may still lead to unexpected delays in payment. Banks move funds through accounts held with each other, keeping track of each other's activities through reconciliation of instructions and advices. All exchanges of currencies have to be settled eventually through accounts held in the countries of those currencies. Thus to change US dollars to Swiss francs and then pay the Swiss francs to Paris requires movements through accounts in New York, Zurich and Paris, as well as the book entries in the bank in London. Not least of the problems associated with cross border flows is that of ensuring that transactions are not attempted on a day when one of the centres involved is on holiday.

The movement of cash has been simplified by a message switching system known as SWIFT, the Society for Worldwide Interbank Financial Telecommunication. SWIFT is a private network with over 1,000 members in 45 countries and was founded in 1973 to provide a fast, secure method for advising various payment-related messages. SWIFT operates a major computer network which transfers messages on standard formats which remove the problems of language and enable the messages to be read by the members' computers and automatically sent or received. The network consists of interface devices in the banks' offices that send messages to country concentrators, similar in function to telephone exchanges, which route the information to a SWIFT switching centre that sends the messages to their final destination through the country concentrators and interface devices involved. SWIFT handles customer and bank-to-bank transfers, foreign exchange, loan and deposit confirmations, collections and special messages, such as statements. Under development are confirmation processes for securities, documentary credits and special payment mechanisms, such as bank cards.

A money transfer instruction to the bank will need to be translated to the SWIFT structure: depending on the normal volume of work, unstructured messages may need to have several hours' grace between receipt and the cut-off time for processing to enable the encoding to take place. A typical SWIFT message is broken into several standard fields, for example, for a MT100 message (one of several types of standardised message), for a single customer transfer the fields, or lines of data, would be as shown in Table 13.1.

Table 13.1   Fields in a MT100 SWIFT message

Field	Description
15	Test key: authentication is usually automatically effected by the receiving bank's interface device.
20	Transaction reference number: up to 16 alpha or numeric characters.
32	Value date, currency code, amount.
50	Ordering customer.
52	Ordering bank: defaults to sending bank.
53	Sender's correspondent bank: the bank which will provide cover to the receiver for the funds to be paid.
54	Receiver's correspondent bank.
57	'Account with' bank: where the beneficiary is to be paid.
59	Beneficiary.
70	Details of payment: up to four lines of 35 characters each. The CHIPS format limits the information given in fields 50, 52, 71 and 72 to 114 characters.
71	Details of charges: who pays, sender or beneficiary.
72	Bank-to-bank information: for example, receiving bank to pay by cheque or telephone advise the beneficiary.

Each line of the message is denoted by the SWIFT field code, which permits automated reading of incoming messages and formatting of outgoing messages. SWIFT has all the problems of a large organisation whose diverse spread of owners makes the introduction of change slow and difficult. It has, however, brought uniformity to the business of money transmission and its standards have to be observed by new entrants to electronic funds transfer, such as CHAPS.

The study of the electronic networks used by the banking system will reward any manager responsible for the movement of cash between one point and another. The network ensures that information can flow in many directions at the same time and for a fractionally larger expense, delays in value dating of receipts and payments can be avoided. This increasing electronic capability makes cash management a major part of treasury management and will mean that the use of electronic equipment becomes a critical element in the effectiveness of the corporate treasurer.

CHAPTER 14

Cash management

Cash movement

The movement of cash is the biggest service that banks provide for their customers. That movement can be active, through, say, a money transfer, passive, through a direct debit, or delayed, through a payment by cheque. Movements can be caused by borrowings against loan facilities or foreign exchange contracts, by randomly timed instructions or by standing orders. The growth of cash management as a subject of great concern for treasury managers reflects the importance of understanding and properly using the money payments system. The study of cash management first began in the US where the geographical limitations placed on banks resulted in a possibly intentionally inefficient money payments system. The techniques developed to solve these problems do not always translate well to Europe and its banking arrangements, but certainly there is a need to develop the same single-minded approach adopted by US companies, which could result in substantial savings. Electronics play an increasingly important role in this area of business.

Movement of money through the banking system is delayed each time a party to that movement is involved. Banks pay each other through a system of correspondents: thus Chase would pay Morgan directly, but may have to route payments to a small bank in West Germany through Morgan's correspondent in, say, Frankfurt.

Each time a correspondent enters the chain then at least one day is taken in additional transmission time. The value of that lost day can be calculated by the following formula.

$$\frac{\text{Amount} \times \text{Days} \times \text{Interest rate}}{\text{Days in year} \times 100}$$

A sum of US $1 million that could be earning us a deposit rate of 10 per cent per annum is worth about US $275 for each calendar day lost in the system; in terms of a working year, of, say, 250 days, rather than a calendar year, this cost rises to US $400. Weekends are expensive.

Funds are moved through cheques, bank drafts, mail transfers and telex. A telex routes the payment through the banking network, as we saw with the

SWIFT transfer mechanism in Chapter 13. A mail transfer is a cheaper, but slower, way of effecting the payment through the same channels of banks and correspondents. Bank drafts are cheques issued by a bank on behalf of its customer and sent directly to the beneficiary; they reduce the time spent in the banking system and reduce the credit risk involved in the payment. As with telex and mail transfers, the payer's account is debited immediately a bank draft is issued, but the beneficiary may have to wait for the postal service to deliver the draft and his own bank to clear the draft. With an ordinary cheque, the payer's account is debited on presentation, while the receiver obtains good value once the cheque has been cleared.

Methods of speeding up cash flow

Cash management techniques were originally concerned with taking back the float that the US banks enjoyed because of the inability of customers to transfer from the branch of a bank in one state to a branch of the same bank in another state. Unless you knew that money was due you had no idea when the receiving bank had collected your funds. Even at 5 per cent per annum, one day's float can soon add up to a substantial sum of money. Control over cash movements could be reduced by buyers paying with cheques drawn on tiny banks in the middle of nowhere, with the resulting delays in presentation and clearance. Sophisticated buyers also researched their banks to select those that had fewest correspondents, so that the routing of documents and payments slowed down even more.

Corporate treasurers on the receiving end fought back with the help of an occasionally reluctant banking system by setting up networks of lock boxes and interception accounts, designed to speed up the flow in the banking system itself, and insisted on customers making payments that followed preselected routes, to remove the haphazard delays caused by using obscure banks. A lock box is a device for speeding up the crediting of payments sent through the mail. Instead of going straight to the beneficiary, the sender is asked to mail the cheque to a lock box address, where the receiver's bank collects the payment and processes it immediately. Techniques such as these are very effective in improving the value dating of funds in the banking network.

Life is complicated by the fact that the federal reserve banks are in competition with commercial banks with regard to clearing services in some respects, so that pricing of cash management services has to take into account the cut-off times of the Fed if the bank involved is to be able to offset the cost of using the Fed system for their customers. As cash managers grew in understanding and in importance among their customers, banks began to introduce electronic assistance, linking the customer directly to the bank. This takes the form of a terminal, connected over the telephone to the bank's operational computer. The services provided by a typical terminal supplied by a bank are extensive and growing in number (see Table 14.1).

These systems report on US-based accounts and some have been extended to include detailed balance reporting from other branches of the reporting bank. Banks outside the US are resisting giving details of balances to their competitors' electronic reporting services, so that the initial use of these terminals

Table 14.1   Electronic cash management capabilities

Service	Present and future capabilities
Information	– detailed bank balance information of account with reporting bank
	– balance history
	– multi-bank consolidation report
	– balance history
	– bank evaluation and account analysis
	– foreign exchange positions and rates
Transactions	– electronic initiation of funds transfer, letters of credit and cheque issuance
	– future services include foreign exchange trades and securities investment
	– transaction investigation
Management	– portfolio management for debt or investment
	– treasury management
	– daily cash book and cash forecasting
Communications	– with time share
	– message system, for example, electronic mail
	– internal hook up to own computers

outside the US has been by multinationals with extensive US business or which use the US financial markets to issue debt instruments.

The most effective way to reduce the time lost in the international banking network is to transfer funds between branches of the same international bank and to use those branches as interception points for funds movements. International payments often involve foreign exchange and it is an interesting observation that companies that expend great energy in shopping around for the cheapest rate for that foreign exchange seem to disregard the additional cost involved in using inefficient payment mechanisms.

Each system has its own specialities. Chase's Infocash, for example, will automatically make transfers in foreign currencies by taking the domestic currency out of the account and arranging the foreign exchange needed without the customer having to call in and settle the rate for every small transaction.

Costs of electronically based products

Banks are aggressively extending electronically based products to their corporate customers in spite of the apparent conflict of providing expensive services at low prices – typically, between US $500 and US $1,500 a month, depending on usage – while allowing customers to become more efficient at the banks' expense. Pressure to provide these services comes from their multinational customers and the banks hope that they will increase substantially their transactional business and use the capacity that is becoming available from the massive investment in computer and communication facilities.

While the US banks created earnings through excesses of float or by encouraging free balances, European banks have had to ensure adequate compensation through charging fees. Thus, in Italy it is not unusual for a quite small company to have as many as 30 banks, so that it can receive payments from the banks of each of its customers without punitive bank transfer charges. In general, the cash manager has been more concerned with interest rates rather than float.

Cash management in Europe is therefore less aggressively pursued by treasurers, reflecting the more cohesive nature of the national banking systems and the greater efficiencies in the services provided. In many ways the US banking system is the worst in the world, but this shortcoming is overlooked in the gloss and clamour of well co-ordinated public images. The problems arise when funds are transferred from one country to another and from one banking system to another.

Time-sharing

The first proponents of international cash management in Europe were the regional headquarters of US multinationals, which realised the cost involved in not using the banking system efficiently. Many of the applications of cash management services relied on using the first methods of accessing the power of a central computer, with banks providing facilities through the time-sharing bureaux such as GEISCO.

The first users of the time-sharing bureaux were the accountants, looking for ways to consolidate the accounts of far-flung subsidiaries in time for reporting deadlines. Each subsidiary was told to enter its results into GEISCO's computer by a certain date and, usually, the accountants would get output in the form of a consolidated set of numbers for head office, while the subsidiary would benefit from having his input recast into the head office format.

Netting systems

Whereas the UK head office treasurer had to contend with the vagaries of the home market, his European counterpart was relatively content with his local markets. He did, however, have a significant problem – the organisation of cross border flows of funds. US multinationals tend to look on Europe as a single market and to adopt a homogeneous approach, while acknowledging some geographical peculiarities do exist. This results in factories set up for political or financial reasons to serve the whole Continent, usually acting as sources for sister factories in other countries or supplying products to overseas sales forces. The first main services provided through a computer terminal by banks were the multilateral netting services run on the time-sharing networks.

Netting systems are designed to reduce the amount of foreign exchange that has to be bought or sold and uses concepts of elegant simplicity. In the simplest situation, a company has two subsidiaries, say, one in France and one in West Germany, who trade with each other by supplying goods and services denominated in their local currencies. Thus, each time the French company settles its debts it has to purchase Deutschmarks and similarly, the West German company must buy French francs. Although both companies may have obtained the finest possible rates for their transactions, the parent company has lost the difference in the spread between bid and offer and in addition to this financial opportunity loss, has exchange rate exposures that may be overstated. By netting out the payments through an agreed rate only a small residual amount of one currency or the other needs to be physically purchased and the profitability of the finished goods is enhanced by the savings in foreign exchange.

More complex applications need a computer to solve the administration required to manage a network of several subsidiaries, each trading with the others to a greater or lesser extent. When mapped out diagrammatically the communications lines look horrendous (see Fig. 14.1).

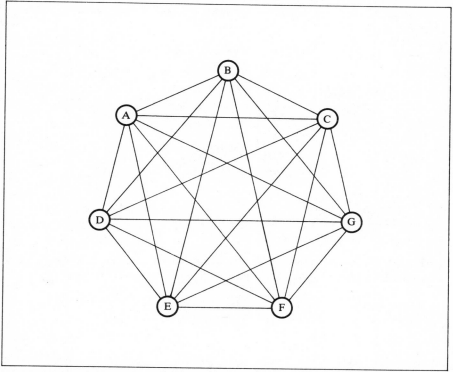

Fig. 14.1   A complex netting system's communications lines

A good analogy for this situation is a telephone exchange: rather than go to the expense and inconvenience of laying lines between every subscriber, the telephone lines all go into a central exchange. With multilateral flows of information the same principles hold good. Put an organisation in the middle to clear the transactions and significant savings in foreign exchange volumes can be made, as well as important improvements in control of activities throughout the corporation (see Fig. 14.2).

Analysis of intercompany payables will show the extent to which savings can be made. Often this is seen in a reduction of as much as 60 per cent of foreign exchange volume. Implementation of a clearing scheme requires considerable start-up effort, all involved must know what has to be done and the resulting benefits. Once set up, the routine is simple and easy to administer.

Each paying company is asked to advise on an agreed date for the amounts

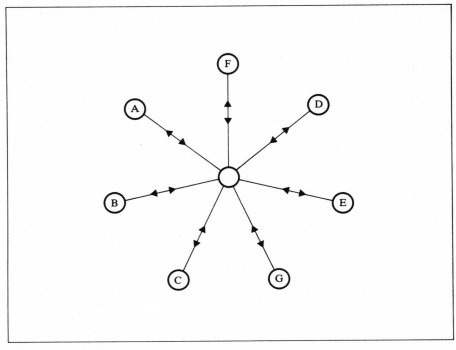

Fig. 14.2   A centralised netting system

and currencies owed to other subsidiary companies. These are then entered on to a matrix and the amounts of foreign exchange are netted out (see Fig. 14.3).

		RECEIVES FROM					
(\$ MILLION)		A	B	C	B	E	TOTAL
	A	0	3	1	0	3	7
	B	1	0	1	3	2	7
PAYS TO	C	3	2	0	2	1	8
	D	1	1	1	0	1	4
	E	2	1	2	2	0	7
	TOTAL	7	7	5	7	7	33
		NET RECEIPTS					
		A	B	C	D	E	TOTAL
	A	0	2	0	0	1	3
NET	B	0	0	0	2	1	3
PAYMENT	C	2	1	0	1	0	4
	D	1	0	0	0	0	1
	E	0	0	1	1	0	2
	TOTAL	3	3	1	4	2	13

Fig. 14.3   Matrix showing amounts and currencies owed

A sum of US $33 million of foreign exchange has been reduced to US $13 million, while 19 funds movements have come down to ten transactions. The US $13 million will be bought or sold centrally, with the benefits of pricing advantage that that amount can command, compared with the piecemeal approach of the individual subsidiaries. Float time in the banking system is minimised and the need to cover forward cash movements is easier to identify and manage.

The computer is needed to co-ordinate flows of information and to compute the amounts needed in various currencies to settle the clearing centre's transactions. It also acts as the payment mechanism to settle the gross flows in and out of each subsidiary's account, which are necessary to book-keeping, but are no longer bank-related entries.

Netting systems can be extended to include third-party payments and receipts. Centralisation of cash flows leads to better co-ordination and controls and a logical progression is to set up a re-invoicing or similar centre further to manage the central treasury function. Here again the computer is instrumental in speeding up the administrative chore.

Centralisation of financial management

Most corporations, whether they are predominantly domestic or international in their trading activities, are made up of a number of companies that engage in a variety of businesses. Even the most decentralised company needs to keep a firm hand on its financial management, to ensure that money is borrowed or invested at the rate that the corporation, rather than the individual company, can obtain. This has resulted in the treasury function acting as a bank to the rest of the group, paying interest on cash surpluses, charging interest on borrowings and transacting foreign exchange at market rates. The centre can thus take positions and manage exposure, using specialists who understand the markets with greater depth than the managers of the subsidiaries. The subsidiaries can still enjoy freedom of timing with regard to when to cover, for example, a forward payment.

Re-invoicing just extends this concept further and centralises the collection and management of intercompany receivables, which can usually be said to be of acceptable creditworthiness and can be delayed or accelerated without an impact in commercial terms on the company's business. Very simply, each subsidiary sends out invoices to its sister companies in the name of the centre, with a copy of the invoice sent to the centre. This has the benefit of allowing subsidiaries effectively to bill each other through the centre in their own currencies, as the centre assumes the foreign exchange exposure that always accompanies a cross currency transaction; the centre, in turn, charges the paying subsidiary in its own currency.

Centralisation enables the corporation to manage its exposures and lead and lag payments to take advantage of expected movements in exchange rates. The corporation can also improve liquidity and operate on a larger scale in the financial markets. As sophistication increases, the company can then use the financial vehicle as an important part of its tax planning, entering the variable of tax efficiency into the central decision making process. While the start-up costs of setting up a re-invoicing centre may be high in terms of computer hardware and communications, the ongoing costs are normally low, as the centre can be run with very few people, with most of the work being fed into the computer by the subsidiaries' computers.

CHAPTER 15

Electronic banking systems

Continuing with the theme of electronic banking, let us look at two systems, one based on a bank's mainframe computers, the other on time-sharing. The examples given come from Citibank and Midland Bank and are widely used by corporations and financial institutions. The electronic banking facilities are similar to those provided by other banks and are at least as advanced as any others on the market. First, however, we will look at some of the electronic banking facilities now on offer to European treasurers.

Facilities available to European treasurers

The first requirement of cash management is to get details of cash balances in a timely manner, to enable good decisions to be made on funding or investing the short-term cash flows arising out of the business. The first level of automation of this process is to replace the daily telephone call with routine telexes from the banks involved. Many European treasurers feel that this is more than adequate for their cash management requirements and certainly most European banks efficiently deliver this information, sometimes in trial balance form by the end of the business day. The next stage of automation is to embrace electronic banking, which is a grand way of describing how to link customer and bank over a data rather than a conversational line.

Most of the major US banks offer electronic banking in some form or another. The race to provide facilities is seen to be both pre-emptive, in the hope that once signed on to a particular bank customers will not sign on with a wide range of competitors, and defensive, to protect existing customers from being seduced away by the attractions of the new technology. The investment is substantial and extends or changes the banks' approaches to the whole area of cash management consultancy. Cash management in Chemical Bank, for example, has virtually been replaced by the all-out marketing of electronic banking systems. Chemical Bank is unusual in that it licenses its software to other banks and has an interesting range of products, made up of ChemLink (electronic banking for corporate customers), BankLink (whereby other banks license ChemLink for their own customers) and Pronto (for home banking). In London, the major US banks all provide electronic banking services, or say that they do, and the clearing banks are entering the market, in one or two cases with packages bought from the US and adapted for the UK.

The main providers of electronic banking are Citibank (through Citibanking), Chase Manhattan (with Infocash), Bank of America (with Bamtrac), Morgan Guaranty (with MARS) and Chemical. Each provides very much the same range of services. Infocash, for example, has on-line reporting of balances and transactions by individual account on a consolidated basis, together with facilities for generating repetitive, standard payments easily. Any treasury manager who needs to watch his cash balances or his foreign exchange exposures benefits enormously from this type of electronic service.

The next stage, which is available in the US and imminent in Europe, will be transaction initiation over the electronic terminals. The customer keys in most of his transaction details and the bank receiving the instruction is well placed to hold down the cost of wages and salaries, as, once entered into the system, the contract will to a greater extent be handled automatically.

Electronic banking terminals are beginning to appear in more and more offices around Europe as the major domestic banks introduce their own versions for their corporate customers. Many of these offerings have been adapted from the software written by US banks or consultants for the US market, amended for language and local regulations in the international markets. Chemical Bank has done well in this area and its BankLink is used by Barclays, Commerzbank, Crédit Lyonnais and the Bank of Scotland, and delivered to their customers through GEISCO's time-sharing facilities. GEISCO provides the benefits of a secure independent carrier for the software, making Chemical Bank's role invisible to the end user.

While Barclays is using BankLink, which took over a year to be adapted to the UK bank's requirements, Midland has been adapting a package from ADP and National Westminster one from NDC; ADP and NDC are the leading software houses in the US which provide cash management services. The time taken to change the basic specifications is the main reason that the UK clearers seem to be slow in getting into the business, but now their products are ready they are becoming noticeably more active. As with Barclays' product, NatWest's network comes over GEISCO and its first products concentrated on balance reporting. While time-sharing may never be as convenient as a dedicated communications network, such as those used by the major US banks, the services advertised by the clearers are reasonably comprehensive.

Although National Westminster's first steps in electronic banking have proved to be somewhat faltering, there is no doubt that the UK banks are making substantial investments in these products. Midland provides a standard range of services, similar to those available from American banks.

Midland's main strengths are in its money transmission services, and its cash management package is designed to make best use of this feature. The electronic banking services include:

1. *Balance reporting.* Reports are available in a choice of formats to suit customer requirements and will show both ledger and cleared positions. The reports can be single or multi-currency, as appropriate.
2. *Transactions details report.* This facility enables the user to view individual credit or debit items or totals passing over the accounts, allowing easier account reconciliation. This feature can also improve credit control.

3. *Uncleared effects.* The items in the course of collection are shown with one- or two-day availability.

4. *Centrally captured clearing totals.* For Midland Bank domestic branch accounts, totals of the automated clearings to be applied to the user's accounts on the current day can be displayed.

5. *Target balance reporting.* This module promotes the optimum utilisation of cash resources. The user sets a target figure for each account which the program will compare with the average daily cleared position. The resultant calculation shows the performance of the account as a surplus or deficit to the target.

6. *Balance history.* This report on an historical format basis enables trend patterns to be established. Data entered up to 60 days previously can be recalled automatically.

7. *Cash flow forecasting.* An in-built simulation model can be used to forecast and assess cash flow projections, thus facilitating the planning of future investment and borrowing needs.

8. *Multinet.* The cost of internal trading can be cut by using Multinet as a netting centre. It is thus an excellent means of improving control within an organisation.

9. *Automated wire transfers.* The treasurer can initiate same-day and forward value transfers in any currency from within his own office using the cash management service to access Midland Bank's payments transmission service.

A typical balance report is shown in Fig. 15.1; a currency account is shown in Fig. 15.2.

```
                        MIDLAND BANK plc
                    BALANCE REPORTING SERVICE
                          REPORT FOR
                          Eurochem PLC
                  Prepared Friday, July 20, 1984
              For Data as of Thursday, July 19, 1984
```

BRANCH/BANK ACCOUNT NUMBER	CURRENCY CODE	LEDGER BALANCE TOTAL CREDITS	CLEARED BALANCE TOTAL DEBITS
MIDLAND BANK plc			
KING ST MANCHESTER 18210167283	GBP	1,454,443.19 Dr 15,473.26	1,462,127.52 Dr 2,000.00
HIGH ST BEDFORD 38031106458	GBP	259,207.23 Cr 106,543.86	259,207.23 Cr 2,470.00
INTERNATIONAL DIV. 00376184	GBP	155,000.00 Cr 5,000.00	152,450.55 Cr 0.00
INTERNATIONAL DIV 68744322	USD	25,000.00 Cr 0.00	25,000.00 Cr 0.00
*****TOTALS*****	GBP	1,040,235.96 Dr 127,017.12	1,050,469.74 Dr 4,470.00
	USD	25,000.00 Cr 0.00	25,000.00 Cr 0.00

```
WAS REPORT RECEIVED OK? (Y OR N) ---Y
```

Fig. 15.1 A typical balance report

```
                    MIDLAND BANK plc
                CASH MANAGEMENT SERVICE
                      REPORT FOR
                     Eurochem PLC
              Prepared Friday, July 20, 1984
          For Data Entered Thursday, July 19, 1984

BRANCH/BANK              CURRENCY        LEDGER BALANCE      CLEARED BALANCE
ACCOUNT NUMBER          CODE            TOTAL CREDITS       TOTAL DEBITS
========================================================================
MIDLAND BANK plc
INTERNATIONAL DIV       USD             5,264,183.64 Dr     5,264,183.64 Dr
68061322                                1,042,540.92          523,983.79


-----------------------------------------------------------------------
    CREDIT AMOUNT              CREDIT DESCRIPTION
-----------------------------------------------------------------------

      8,001.24                B/O BCO URQIJO HISPANO         19 JUL 84
    118,518.81                STANDARD CHARTERED 007925      19 JUL 84
    503,998.21                STANDARD CHARTERED BK 7941     19 JUL 84
    200,204.57                STANDARD CHARTERED BK 7943     19 JUL 84
    201,831.30                STANDARD CHARTERED BK LONDON   19 JUL 84
      9,986.79                64 311106                      19 JUL 84


-----------------------------------------------------------------------
    DEBIT AMOUNT               DEBIT DESCRIPTION
-----------------------------------------------------------------------

    168,142.12                182548 OUR SALE STG 93200      19 JUL 84
        22.80                 52TT2409C00186CHGS             19 JUL 84
     79,216.75                CH/26450/UK 9A/22226           19 JUL 84
     82,901.25                CH/26450/UK 9A/22226           19 JUL 84
    193,700.87                52/2709C00156                  19 JUL 84
========================================================================

WAS THE REPORT RECEIVED OK? (Y OR N)----Y
```

Fig. 15.2   A typical currency account

Clearing banks offer a different service in some ways, using their branch network to create domestic as well as international cash management systems. Thus, the source of the information is as important as the presentation of the service.

One of the attractions of electronic banking is that it offers the potential implementation of the key improvement to productivity provided by computers, the single entry of data into a system. If the customer authorises a transaction by entering the instruction himself into the electronic banking terminal, then no confirming letters are needed, while the bank can pass the instruction through its processing virtually untouched by human hand. The more transactions the customer has with that particular bank, the easier it will be to integrate the customer's mainframe with the bank's computers. Using an intelligent terminal, the customer can achieve much of that synergy with several banks, as the terminal will distribute the information created by the electronic instruction automatically to the mainframe as required.

The first electronic packages offered in London were little more than US systems transposed to Europe or terminals which hooked into cash management systems in the US and of interest only to those companies with US subsidiaries. Initial reaction was therefore somewhat sceptical and did little to change the European treasurers' natural lack of interest in the whole topic of cash management. Now that these systems have been fairly thoroughly overhauled, the solutions offered have more relevance to European companies and are arousing more interest.

Services offered by banks' mainframe computers

An electronic banking service provides terminal-based access to the customer's personal data held in the international branches of the bank involved. The data available covers account details – balances and statements for at least the previous month – as well as information on transactions concerning loans, deposits and foreign exchange, again with historical records. Let us look at Citibanking through typical screens available to an imaginary customer, 'Eurochem', which has a well developed relationship with the bank and uses a wide range of banking products. It is connected to the service through a modem. After keying into its terminal, the password that allows it access to its account details a simple code word that takes it either into product enquiry, treasury management or, in the near future, transaction initiation. Let us first look at the account balances in summary detail (see Fig. 15.3).

```
================================================================================
CITIBANK LONDON              BALANCE SUMMARY
                            ----------------
CUSTOMER       8000537714                 EUROCHEM
--------------------------------------------------------------------------------
ACCOUNT NR.    A/C TYPE            CCY       AS OF      LEDGER BALANCE
--------------------------------------------------------------------------------
     5178      COMPOSITE          GBP     05 NOV.83       34,053.75
    31239      CURRENT            GBP     05 NOV.83          751.96
    54784      DEPOSIT            GBP     02 NOV.83       39,222.61
   612325      CURRENT            USD     05 NOV.83    1,065,748.43
  5367913      DEPOSIT            USD     05 NOV.83        5,494.13




**************************************************************INFORMATION AS OF 06 NOV.83
06 NOV.83    TIME    09 03 04                    PAGE 001/001   LAST PAGE
======)
```

Fig. 15.3   Account balances of Eurochem

The screen shown in Fig. 15.3 shows the ledger balance, which includes all entries passed over the account up to the date shown and may not be the same amount that is available to be withdrawn as cash at this time, as some entries may not be receiving value until some time in the future. Currencies are shown in SWIFT type codes, with the first two letters denoting the country and the third letter the currency unit. The 'AS OF' column shows the date of the last movement on each of the five accounts. A composite account from Citibank is one that combines the features of current and deposit accounts and can have overdrafts and cheque books, as well as paying interest on credit balances. Let us look at details of the first account shown by selecting '1', the reference at the end of the first line: our choice would be shown against the arrow on the very bottom line of the page. This takes us into a screen showing the account statement (see Fig. 15.4).

```
==================================================================================
CITIBANK LONDON          ACCOUNT STATEMENT   COMPOSITE AC              5178
----------------------------------------------------------------------------------
CUSTOMER        8000537714              EUROCHEM
----------------------------------------------------------------------------------
DATE       NARRATIVE              REFERENCE     VALUE   CCY        AMOUNT
----------------------------------------------------------------------------------
05 NOV. 83 OPENING BALANCE                              GBP        881,657.51
           DEPOSIT                              07 NOV.            159,330.07
           CCY PMNT ORDER         0001794168    05 NOV.            24,893.19
           DEPOSIT                              07 NOV.            10,000.00
           ISSUE  BANKERS PMNT    0001796907    05 NOV.          1,000,006.00-
           DRAFT ISSUED           0001794394    05 NOV.            41,809.02-
           ISSUE  BANKERS PMNT    0001796908    05 NOV.                12.00-
05 NOV. 83 CLOSING BALANCE                              GBP        35,053.75
```

```
**************************************************************INFORMATION AS OF 06 NOV. 83
06 NOV. 83    TIME    09 03 04                        PAGE 001/001    LAST PAGE
=======)
```

Fig. 15.4   Account statement of Eurochem

We are looking at a fairly active account, that combines the features of an overdraft facility with an interest bearing non-fixed maturity deposit account: standing orders, cheque books and all the other services associated with an operating account can be used. Omnibus accounts such as these are a simple first step to active cash management, as the penalty for not investing cash surpluses is offset by the interest paid on credit balances, which can also be used to pay for banking services. Eurochem could have asked for statements for up to 45 days' previous activity by entering a different request code rather than moving through the screens from one page to another. By keying '2' we can look at the detail behind the third entry on the account statement (see Fig. 15.5).

```
==================================================================================
CITIBANK LONDON                   CREDIT ADVICE       YOUR REF:
CUSTOMER       8000537714                NAME EUROCHEM
----------------------------------------------------------------------------------
WE HAVE CREDITED YOUR  ACCT              5178         AS FOLLOWS:

VALUE          05 NOV. 83        CURRENCY/AMOUNT  GBP              24,893.19
                                                  ==============================
DETAILS
   FUNDS TRANSFER RECEIVED/OUR REF.      0001794168

CURRENCY AMOUNT/RECVD.                            BEF              2,022,694

   CONVERTED AT THE RATE OF   81.2549000          GBP              24,893.19
```

```
****************************************************************BOOKED ON 05 NOV. 83
06 NOV. 83 TIME    09 11 19                           PAGE 001/001  ))))
======)
```

Fig. 15.5   Details of the account statement

The '>>>>' show that more information is available by pressing the enter key on the terminal (see Fig. 15.6).

```
===================================================================================
CITIBANK LONDON          PAYMENT TRANSACTION DETAILS          REF      0001794168
                         -----------------------------
CUSTOMER    8000537714                        NAME EUROCHEM
-----------------------------------------------------------------------------------
THE FOLLOWING TRANSFER HAS BEEN RECEIVED FOR YOUR ACCT        5178

VALUE       05 NOV. 83        CURRENCY/AMOUNT  BEF              2.022,694
                                               =================================
ORDERING BANK                          DETAILS OF PAYMENT
  CITIBANK (BELGIUM) SA                 CBL FM CITIBANK BRUSSELS
                                        O/O DATACHEM
                                        REF MO61F 210.278-405-440-312-
                                        313-441-121509
```

```
**********************************************************************BOOKED ON 05 NOV. 83
06 NOV. 83 TIME    09 12 19                      PAGE 002/002 LAST PAGE
======)
```

Fig. 15.6   Payment transaction details

Ledger balances may be essential for book-keeping, but are unhelpful for cash managers, who need to see what funds are available today or on future days. The electronic banking facility provides a cash availability forecast based on the transactions that have been recorded against one or several accounts. Let us look at the composite account 5178 and see the cash balances listed in value date order, showing when funds can be used or invested (see Fig. 15.7).

```
CITIBANK LONDON          CASH AVAIL. PROJECTION FOR A/C        5178
                         -------------------------------------------------
CUSTOMER    8000537714                        NAME EUROCHEM
-----------------------------------------------------------------------------------
DETAILS                  VALUE    CCY              AMOUNT           ENTRY DATE
-----------------------------------------------------------------------------------
AVAILABLE BALANCE        06 NOV. 83  GBP        -135,276.32
DEPOSIT                  07 NOV. 83             159,330.07         05 NOV. 83
DEPOSIT                  07 NOV. 83              10,000.00         05 NOV. 83
                         07 NOV. 83        ********34,053.75
```

```
*****************************************INFORMATION FROM    06 NOV. 83-13 NOV. 83
06 NOV. 83 TIME   10 47 31                       PAGE 001/001 LAST PAGE))
======)
```

Fig. 15.7   Cash balances listed in value date order

We can see that the credit ledger balance of 6 November is in fact a negative cash amount that will attract overdraft charges unless it is balanced out. This statement does not include items that have not yet been booked on to the account, although contracts exist on the bank's books that will pass over the account at a later date. This information can also be called up easily (see Fig. 15.8).

Information can be ordered or arranged to meet the user's needs. Although this is the last page of this statement, the '>>' at the bottom right of the page signify that we can look at the next account by pressing the enter key, without having to re-enter the access code to get that particular screen (see Fig. 15.9).

```
========================================================================
CITIBANK LONDON            CASH AVAIL.PROJECTION FOR A/C        5178
------------------------------------------------------------------------
CUSTOMER    8000537714               NAME EUROCHEM
------------------------------------------------------------------------
DETAILS                 VALUE    CCY              AMOUNT       ENTRY DATE
------------------------------------------------------------------------
AVAILABLE BALANCE     06 NOV.83  GBP           -135,276.32
DEPOSIT               07 NOV.83                 159,330.07     05 NOV.83
DEPOSIT               07 NOV.83                  10,000.00     05 NOV.83
                      07 NOV.83              ********34,053.75
FX SOLD               08 NOV.83                 100,000.00
                      08 NOV.83              *******134,053.75



*****************************************INFORMATION FROM     06 NOV.83-13 NOV.83
06 NOV.83 TIME 10 47 31                            PAGE 001/001 LAST PAGE>>
======>
```

Fig. 15.8   Updated payment transaction details

```
========================================================================
CITIBANK LONDON            CASH AVAIL. PROJECTION SUMMARY
------------------------------------------------------------------------
CUSTOMER    8000537714               NAME EUROCHEM
------------------------------------------------------------------------
VALUE DATES        06 NOV.83      07 NOV.83     08 NOV.83      11 NOV.83
------------------------------------------------------------------------
GBP NET POS         -40,900        168,952       292,498       292,498
    OUTFLOW
.........................................................................
USD NET POS      -1,071,243         49,118        52,000        52,000
    OUTFLOW                         50,000



========================================================================
GBP TOTAL          -633,140        196,108       321,246       321,246
*************************************************************************
06 NOV.83 TIME   10 58 29                       PAGE 001/001  >>>>>>>>>>>
```

Fig. 15.9   Net available cash balances on sterling and US dollar accounts

We can view the net available cash balances on all Eurochem's sterling and US dollar accounts, day by day, with a total on the bottom expressed in the currency of choice, in this case sterling. The second US dollar entry, on 7 November for US $50,000, reports a cash movement, probably due to a maturing foreign exchange or deposit contract that has yet to be allocated to any particular account.

We can go on to the next page of this report by pressing the enter key (see Fig. 15.10).

We could have asked for cash availability on a specific date for each of the next four months, for the funds movement caused by US dollar foreign exchange or money market transactions on a particular day or for any of several other projections. We could ask for maturity schedules of all foreign exchange, deposit and loan contracts or obtain schedules for each type of contract.

Let us see what we could do with the information relating to foreign exchange contracts. The data can be presented in a very raw state as a simple listing of all contracts maturing between 19 November and 22 November (see Fig. 15.11).

```
===========================================================================
CITIBANK LONDON        CASH AVAIL.  PROJECTION SUMMARY
-------------------------------------------------------------------------
CUSTOMER     8000537714                 NAME EUROCHEM
-------------------------------------------------------------------------
VALUE DATES      12 NOV. 83       13 NOV. 83    30 NOV. 83
-------------------------------------------------------------------------
GBP NET POS        192, 498         392, 498      405, 800
    OUTFLOW
. . . . . . . . . . . . . . . . . . . . . . . . . . . . . . . . . . . . . . . .
USD NET POS         52, 000          52, 000       52, 000
    OUTFLOW
```

```
===========================================================================
GBP TOTAL          221, 246         421, 246      434, 548
***************************************************************************
06 NOV.83  TIME 10 58 35                      PAGE 002/002    LAST PAGE
======)
```

Fig. 15.10   Cash availability on specific dates

```
===========================================================================
CITIBANK LONDON           FOREIGN EXCHANGE SUMMARY
                          --------------------------------
CUSTOMER     8000537714                 NAME EUROCHEM
-------------------------------------------------------------------------
REFERENCE    CCY           AMOUNT    CCY        AMOUNT         VALUE
-------------------------------------------------------------------------
**BOUGHT**
1000921296   USD        80, 956. 10  GBP     43, 000. 00    21 NOV. 83   1
1000948354   USD     1, 149, 687. 00 GBP    630, 000. 00    21 NOV. 83   2
1000987182   USD       524, 356. 00  GBP    280, 000. 00    19 NOV. 83   3
1001038326   USD       910, 700. 00  GBP    500, 000. 00    19 NOV. 83   4
***SOLD***
1000933387   USD       646, 205. 00  GBP    350, 000. 00    21 NOV. 83   5
1000934293   USD       625, 090. 00  GBP    340, 000. 00    21 NOV. 83   6
1000965719   USD     2, 827, 500. 00 GBP  1, 500, 000. 00   21 NOV. 83   7
*ARBITRAGE*  ********BOUGHT**********    ***********SOLD********
1000921520   FRF       447, 200. 00  USD     80, 000. 00    21 NOV. 83   8
1000986684   FRF     3, 053, 400. 00 USD    525, 000. 00    19 NOV. 83   9
1001007389   USD     2, 210, 583. 59 FRF  13, 000, 000. 00  22 NOV. 83  10
1000942190   USD       500, 000, 00  JPY  109, 675, 000     19 NOV. 83  11
***************************************************************************
06 NOV.83 TIME  09:36:10                      PAGE 001/001    LAST PAGE
======)
```

Fig. 15.11   Contracts maturing between specific dates

Contracts are shown in the order they were booked in and are listed in US dollar/sterling bought and sold, with a separate listing for foreign exchange involving other currencies.

Let us look at the yen/US dollar transaction, deal number 11 (see Fig. 15.12).

The information shown is the bank's own media confirming the transaction, which is therefore described in the bank's terms. These are the other way around from the entry on the foreign exchange summary (see Fig. 15.11) which is laid out in the customer's terms.

We need to know what Eurochem's positions are, because again the raw data does not analyse its cash requirements or its foreign exchange exposures. We move through to another screen (see Fig. 15.13).

We can see the foreign exchange exposures that have resulted from the contracts shown in the foreign exchange summary in Fig. 15.11. For example, the sterling/US dollar exposure of US $4,098,795 shown for 21 November is the sum of the contracts labelled 5, 6 and 7 on that screen, with the resulting

```
================================================================================
CITIBANK LONDON           FOREIGN EXCHANGE CONTRACT       REF        1000942190
                          -------------------------
CUSTOMER    8000537714                    NAME EUROCHEM
--------------------------------------------------------------------------------
WE CONFIRM THE FOREIGN EXCHANGE DEAL 15 JUL.83

AMOUNT BOUGHT JPY       109,675,000  AMOUNT SOLD   USD              500,000.00
================================================================================
RATE    219.3500000000          VALUE    19 NOV.83

ON MATURITY YOU WILL REMIT TO OUR ACCOUNT WITH
CITIBANK TOKYO

ON MATURITY WE WILL REMIT TO YOUR ACCOUNT WITH
CITIBANK NEW YORK



********************************************************************************
06 NOV.83  TIME    09 37 49
======)
```

Fig. 15.12   Foreign exchange deal number 11

```
================================================================================
CITIBANK LONDON           FX MATURITY ANALYSIS
                          --------------------
CUSTOMER    8000537714                    NAME EUROCHEM
--------------------------------------------------------------------------------
VALUE      CCY     NET AMOUNT BOUGHT CCY     NET AMOUNT SOLD        AV. RATE
--------------------------------------------------------------------------------
19 NOV.83  FRF      3,053,400.00  USD          525,000.00          5.816000
           USD      1,435,056.00  GBP          780,000.00          1.847050
           USD        500,000.00  JPY      109,675,000           219.350000
21 NOV.83  GBP      2,190,000.00  USD        4,098,795.00          1.856600
           FRF        447,200.00  USD           80,000.00          5.590000
           USD      1,230,643.10  GBP          673,000.00          1.853800
22 NOV.83  USD      2,210,583.59  FRF       13,000,000.00          5.880800

TOTAL--------------BOUGHT----------------------SOLD----------------------NET
FRF        3,500,600.00  FRF       13,000,000.00            9,499,400.00-
USD        5,376,282.69  USD        4,703,795.00              672,487.69
GBP        2,190,000.00  GBP        1,453,000.00              737,000.00
JPY                   0  JPY          109,675,000           109,675,000-

*****************************************MATURITY DATES FROM 19 NOV.83 - 22 NOV.83
06 NOV.83  TIME    11 16 15                      PAGE 001/001    LAST PAGE
======)
```

Fig. 15.13   Cash requirements and foreign exchange exposures

average rate. The aggregate US dollar exposure for the period, however, is about US $675,000 long. If it is necessary to convert this surplus into another currency to settle other transactions, that conversion may be effected now rather than later, depending on the view of future exchange rates. As a UK-based company Eurochem may not be concerned with anything other than its sterling position against these other currencies and it could have retrieved its information to meet that requirement.

A regional manager could get information from most of the bank's European branches by dialling them directly and he could easily determine overall group exposure before taking action unilaterally, as it is quite possible that the group's overall position counterbalances the local position that he is worried about.

A system based on time-sharing

Treasurers also have to manage portfolios of borrowings and securities, an integral part of the company's funding, investment income and liquidity profile. The second system we will look at is a treasury management tool which helps solve this problem. The CitiTreasury Manager (CTM) is again the outcome of the needs of the US treasurer, who tends to invest in a wider range of instruments than his European counterpart. The CTM is an information system that holds data on loans, investments and foreign exchange, generates reports and confirmation letters, and provides analysis based on the value or valuation of the portfolio. Once again a single entry enables all these tasks to be performed.

The CTM is a terminal-based system, accessing a time-sharing computer over a telephone line. Once information has been entered, the program determines the amount of interest to be paid or received and calculates yields. Reports can be generated to provide whatever arrangements of information are required, in a similar way to the electronic banking facility described earlier. Where the host bank is acting as the issuing agent for certificates of deposit or commercial paper in the US, the CTM can be used to pass instructions directly to the department concerned, without any need for telephone or written instructions or worry over the time difference between the US and Europe.

The following list shows the type of reports generated on cash flow, inventory, income/expense, market value and performance and yield.
1. Cash flow – consolidates all cash movements arising out of the facilities held in inventory and shows inflows and outflows on a daily basis.
2. Inventory – provides a summary or detailed report of all facilities outstanding on the CTM on a consolidated or a daily basis.
3. Income/expense – shows the income or expense associated with one of a group of facilities and the amounts to be accrued on a daily basis of the cost or income involved.
4. Market value – prices securities based on current market rates and shows the profit and loss against the previous valuation.
5. Performance/yield – reports by specified time periods the average weighted maturities and yields for the portfolio by main product groups.
6. Security transaction history.

As the availability of telephone connections increases, so accessing time-sharing computers has improved. Using a properly installed modem, dialling is quick and the access to the computer secure. Let us use the CTM as an example of a time-sharing computer (see Fig. 15.14).

Once we get through to the computer facility we are asked to walk through three sets of passwords, one for the computer itself, one to identify the company and the third to identify the individual. Once in, the computer responds by name 'HELLO LORI PINTO' and gives the menu selection (the choice of options available). We now print 'H' and put in a new deal.

We can correct any line that we need to and when we are satisfied by the entry, we can look at the log of the transaction (see Figs. 15.15 and 15.16). When we are satisfied that the log is correct, we can enter the deal into the data base of the system. The program is menu-driven, so that the user is stepped through gently from one part of the program to another. If required, each entry of transactional data can be used to generate a confirmation letter containing

```
CITIBANK, CITI OF TOMORROW
44.123
WELCOME TO CITIBANK LONDON, PLEASE SELECT THE SERVICE REQUIRED
CITI TREASURY MANAGER


ENTER PASSWORD, USERID
00000000

HELLO LORI PINTO

** MAIN MENU **

SELECT OPTION

  1 - ACCES - ACCESS CONTROL
  2 - CNFRM - CONFIRMATION INTERFACE
  3 - CUSTO - CUSTOMIZATION
  4 - ENTRY - ENTRY
  5 - MODIF - MODIFICATION
  6 - PASSW - PASSWORD CHANGE
  7 - REPOR - REPORTS
  8 - SALES - SALE TRANSACTION
  9 - UPDAT - UPDATE TRANSACTION
 10 - XMESG - MESSAGES
SELECT OPTION
```

Fig. 15.14   Accessing the computer

```
** TRANSACTION ENTRY **

ENTER PORTFOLIO, TYPE
  LAD, CO
ENTER ISSUER
  CITI
ENTER DEALER
  BECKER
ENTER COUNTRY OR STATE
  US
ENTER CURRENCY
  US
ENTER ISSUE DATE, NOMINAL RATE, ISSUE AMOUNT
  110183, 9.5, 1000000
ENTER SETTLEMENT DATE, EFFECTIVE RATE
  110883, 9.125
ENTER MATURITY DATE
  10384
TYPE "A" FOR AUTOMATIC ACCEPTANCE

MOVE PAGE TO BREAK AND HIT RETURN OR "LIST"
```

Fig. 15.15   Transaction entry

the details of the transaction. The user can define the portfolio and the types of securities he wants to inspect by any of the headings that the instruments are filed under, such as the issuer or currency.

Some sample reports are shown in Figs. 15.17 and 15.18. The first is a cash flow report that gives a calendar of all inflows and outflows of transactions booked on the system (see Fig. 15.17). The second report shows a portfolio inventory (see Fig. 15.18). A summary performance report combines several reports, for portfolio inventory, expenses, income, etc., and again is available for any time period required (see Fig. 15.19).

The use of these systems can be extended by using imagination to apply them to existing problems. The CTM can be used very effectively to surmount the communications problems that the dealer has in putting together a transaction using US dollar bankers' acceptances with a sterling swap. The New York office

```
TRANSACTION LOG
---------------
```

```
    PORTFOLIO: ASSET DEMO PORTFOLIO       INSTRUMENT: CERTIFICATE OF DEPOSIT

 4) ISSUER: CITI                    5) DEALER: BECKER

22) CURRENCY: US

50) NOMINAL RATE:    9.5000000

51) EFFECTIVE RATE:    9.1250000

          (1)  DATE    (2) PRINCIPAL      (3) INTEREST       (4) TOTAL
60) ISSUE      11/ 1/83  1,000,000.00
70) SETTLEMENT 11/ 8/83  1,000,549.32         1,847.22     1,002,396.54
80) MATURITY    1/ 3/84  1,000,000.00        16,625.00     1,016,625.00

HIT RETURN IF CORRECT OR NUMBER TO CHANGE, "L" TO LIST
```

```
*** TRANSACTION 002808 ACCEPTED ***

ENTER PORTFOLIO TYPE
```

Fig. 15.16   Transaction log

can keep the bankers' acceptance rates on-line in the CTM and London can access them and create the transaction without the need for telephone or telex contact. All the necessary book-keeping entries can be generated at each end for transmission to the back office, which is no longer under time pressure to turn the work around.

Time-sharing solves the problem of getting remote locations to work together. The overall exchange rate exposure of the corporation can be determined by using a time-sharing network. The treasurer can ask the financial managers in each subsidiary regularly to report their projected balance sheets, and foreign currency transactions and exposures can be calculated on any basis, for example, pre-tax or after-tax; the treasurer can then determine whether or not to hedge certain transactions from a corporate point of view or to hedge the balance sheets of subsidiaries to protect himself against currency movements that reduce the value of those balance sheets in terms of the parent company.

All of these electronic banking services exist to help the customer – certainly they do very little to help the banks who are taking a very long-term view on the massive investments they are making in this area. Treasurers should be becoming familiar with these products, particularly as some are so new that they could be changed to give specific benefit to the company with very little extra effort from the bank involved. Once the service is standardised, these changes will be difficult to achieve.

CITI TREASURY MANAGER   G.C.M. CORPORATION
09/02/83   CASH FLOW REPORT (IN THOUSANDS)
CURRENCY:US

PORTFOLIOS: DINV

SECURITIES: ALL

(ALL ACTIVITY)

FROM: 01/01/83   TO: 12/31/83

	JAN	FEB	MAR	APR	MAY	JUN	JUL	AUG	SEP	OCT	NOV	DEC
1	SAT				SUN			116		SAT		SAT
2	SUN			SAT						SUN		SUN
3				SUN					SAT			SAT
4						SAT			SUN			SUN
5		SAT	SAT			SUN					SAT	
6		SUN	SUN					SAT			SUN	
7				-1958	SAT		2000	SUN				
8	SAT			SAT	SUN -2050	1000				SAT		SAT
9	SUN			SUN			SAT			SUN		SUN
10							SUN		SAT			SAT
11						SAT			SUN			SUN
12		SAT	SAT			SUN					SAT	
13		SUN	SUN					SAT			SUN	
14			48		SAT			SUN	48			
15	SAT				SUN		SAT			SAT		
16	SUN		-2505	SAT		2069	SUN			SUN		
17				SUN	-1520				SAT			SAT
18						SAT			SUN			SUN
19		SAT	SAT			SUN					SAT	
20		SUN	SUN					SAT			SUN	
21					SAT			SUN				
22	SAT				SUN		SAT			SAT		
23	SUN			SAT			SUN			SUN		
24				SUN					SAT			SAT
25						SAT			SUN			SUN
26		SAT	SAT			SUN					SAT	
27		SUN	SUN					SAT			SUN	
28		XXX			SAT			SUN				
29	SAT	XXX			SUN	1535	SAT			SAT		
30	SUN	XXX		SAT			SUN			SUN	XXX	
31		XXX		XXX		XXX	SAT		XXX		XXX	SAT
TOTAL			-2457	-1958	-3571	4604	2000	116	48			

Fig. 15.17   Calendar of inflows and outflows

```
INVENTORY REPORT                    09/02/83                    PAGE 1

                    G.C.M.  CORPORATION
                    AS OF: 06/30/83

PORTFOLIOS: DINV
SECURITIES: ALL
```

DESCRIPTION / PORTF / TYPE	SETTLEMT DATE	PAR VALUE	MATURITY DATE	MATURITY VALUE	QUOTED YIELD	EFFECT YIELD	PCT OF TOTAL
GCM CORP. INVESTMENTS							
US GOVERNMENT - - BECKER - / 000348 US DINV TB	04/07/83	2,000,000.00	07/07/83	2,000,000.00	8.3700	8.5509	34.8
US GOVERNMENT - - BECKER - / 000344 US DINV TN	03/17/83	2,500,000.00	01/31/85	2,615,625.00	9.2500	9.7985	43.5
CREDIT SUISSE - - CIBL - / 000346 SF DINV EBD	06/06/83	3,250,000.00	05/31/85	3,404,375.00	4.7500	4.2130	100.0
SHELL INT.FINANCE - - CIBL - / 000341 US DINV BD	03/15/77	1,250,000.00	03/15/87	1,298,437.50	7.7500	7.7500	21.7
DEUTSCHE BANK - - CIBL - / 000345 DM DINV EBD	01/19/83	3,000,000.00	05/01/87	3,255,000.00	8.5000	7.2244	100.0
TOTAL US		5,750,000.00		5,914,062.50		8.9192 / 8.9839	100.0
TOTAL SF		3,250,000.00		3,404,375.00		4.2130 / 4.2716	100.0
TOTAL DM		3,000,000.00		3,255,000.00		7.2244 / 7.3247	100.0
GRAND TOTAL US		5,750,000.00		5,914,062.50		8.9192 / 8.9839	100.0
GRAND TOTAL SF		3,250,000.00		3,404,375.00		4.2130 / 4.2716	100.0
GRAND TOTAL DM		3,000,000.00		3,255,000.00		7.2244 / 7.3247	100.0

Fig. 15.18   A portfolio inventory

PERFORMANCE REPORT   09/02/83   PAGE 1

DATE: 06/01/83 TO 07/01/83

PORTFOLIOS: DINV
SECURITIES: ALL

	PURCHASED		HOLDINGS			END OF PERIOD	
SECURITY (SE)	WEIGHTED AV. MATURITY	W. AVG. YIELD	WEIGHTED AV. MATURITY	W. AVG. YIELD	AVERAGE DAILY BALANCE	WEIGHTED AV. MATURITY	BALANCE
BONDS (US)	0.00	0.00	3652.00	7.86	1,250,000.00	1354.00	1,250,000.00
CERTIFICATE OF DEPOSIT (US)	0.00	0.00	38.57	8.76	2,563,283.38	0.00	0.00
TREASURY BILL (US)	0.00	0.00	120.51	9.16	2,208,173.89	7.00	1,957,658.00
TREASURY NOTES (US)	0.00	0.00	686.00	9.80	2,505,246.55	581.00	2,505,246.55
SUMMARY (US)	0.00	0.00	662.27	9.04	8,526,703.82	553.44	5,712,931.55
EURO BOND (SF)	725.00	4.27	725.00	4.27	2,737,203.42	701.00	3,284,644.10
SUMMARY (SF)	725.00	4.27	725.00	4.27	2,737,203.42	701.00	3,284,644.10
EURO BOND (DM)	0.00	0.00	1563.00	7.32	3,317,750.00	1401.00	3,317,750.00
TIME DEPOSIT (DM)	0.00	0.00	92.00	5.32	500,000.00	0.00	0.00
SUMMARY (DM)	0.00	0.00	1291.78	7.06	3,817,750.00	1401.00	3,317,750.00

Fig. 15.19   A summary performance report

CHAPTER 16

Computer security

As the size of computers comes down, the direct involvement of managers with them will go up. It is no coincidence that managers who are knowledgeable about computers and take an interest in them get a far superior service from the data processing department. Every desk will soon have a computer of some sort upon it and managers should form at first-hand their own evaluations of the merits of one system compared with another. If the purchasing decision falls on the financial manager this evaluation will be all the more critical, as he will only have himself to blame if the purchase is a bad one.

Operational security

Operational security is the first consideration. Is the computer compatible with other computers in the company, is software interchangeable, can it be made to communicate with the mainframe? More importantly, once a decision is made to buy a particular system, will it get proper service and maintenance, will the supplier be around in a year's time – it is still that sort of business – or, an equally critical consideration, will the manufacturer still be supporting the hardware? There is no need to be passive with regard to the structure and specification of the hardware that will make up the system or in the selection of storage media.

Commercial security

Hand-in-hand with the introduction of computerisation comes the problem of commercial security. This falls into two areas, the protection of information and the prevention of fraud, including the theft of software.

Protection of information

As communications improve, so does access to computer systems by un-authorised people. Wilful acts of vandalism by disaffected employees is one of the major causes of computer malfunctions or loss of data. Significantly, most senior managers do not consider that this is a major problem, a view not shared by auditors or technical staff who are closer to the problem.

A fair number of these problems can be managed by taking physical pre-cautions. An obvious step is to keep back-up copies of all important material in a different site from the computer facility and to keep copies of software securely in a safe, preferably a fire-proof safe. Passwords to access computers should be changed frequently and simple things, like checking up on what people are doing, will prevent most problems.

A feature of technology is the growth of groups of people who simply want to show themselves that they can beat or manipulate the system. In the 1970s, the most common manifestation of this were the 'phone phreaks', who spent their waking hours finding ways to get around the international telephone network for no charge. By producing the tones that work the telephone system they were able to make calls to thousands of miles away. Equally subtle ploys were used in the UK to make free calls on the STD. Apart from some rather sinister interest from the Mafia, the activity seems fairly good-natured and harmless – after all what much else is there to do after you have said 'hello'? Only the telephone companies suffered and they were well able to take care of themselves and prevent this from happening in the future.

Home computer buffs are the phreaks of the 1980s and while they may not get the spectacular results depicted in the motion picture *War Games* (where a young boy with a home computer nearly starts the third world war), they can cause considerable damage. Unlike the telephone phreaks they can be anti-social, by getting into private data bases and giving instructions to other computers. Time-sharing bureaux have up to now been the most vulnerable, as they rely on telecommunications. An early case, reported in 1974, involved a schoolboy who used his school's terminal to get into a time-sharing computer and watch how files were accessed to get hold of privileged passwords. He was then free to look at anything held on the computer. As communication links grow, so the computers owned by individual companies are now exposed to this sort of interference. Three schoolboys in New York recently used their school computer to get into the Tymnet international communications network and found their way into Pepsi Cola's Canadian message system. As a result truckloads of bottles of drinks were sent from one end of the country to another on unauthorised journeys. It took the FBI and the Royal Canadian Mounted Police three weeks to track down and catch the culprits.

Equally spectacular have been the exploits of a gang known as the 414s, young boys who used their home computers and telephones to get into Telenet, the network run by the GTE Corporation. Telenet is a time-sharing computer bureau and is used by companies and institutions to hold data bases that are common to several users. The 414s waited around in the system and overheard the codes used to access the data held on several different computers. Fortunately they had little interest other than in just breaking in, but the list of companies broken into was impressive and included a cement company, a cancer research centre, the Security Pacific Bank in Los Angeles and Los Alamos, the research laboratory for nuclear weapons.

Fraud

Theft is a serious problem. Some of it is the equivalent of taking pens and paperclips home from the office. This is the unauthorised use of the company's computers by operators who provide a data processing service to private clients. This is a fairly common misuse of company property and is usually accompanied by sudden increases in overtime, a second hit for the company.

Serious computer fraud is a new field of human endeavour. Not unexpectedly it is the banks that have had the most attention, because those are the places where money and computers come together. The surprisingly few cases of computer crime that are brought to the courts may indicate that it is more difficult to accomplish than seems at first sight or that the criminals are too clever to be found by the company's security system or by the police. In the US, the first computer frauds were carried out by young programmers who seemed to be happy with exerting considerable ingenuity for scant reward. In one case an employee instructed the computer to ignore his personal overdraft and he was only found out when the computer broke down and the overdrafts had to be processed by hand. The bank was so impressed that after firing him it rehired him as a consultant. There is a story from another bank of a 20-year-old programmer who transfered US $100 from 41 different accounts to one opened in a fictitious name. The bank only permitted withdrawals of US $500 a day and it took so long to get the money out of the bank that the crime surfaced, was traced to the programmer and he and his wife were caught taking out part of the proceeds of the fraud.

Nowadays the thefts are of a different order of magnitude. Wells Fargo in Los Angeles lost over US $21 million between 1980 and 1981 to a computer fraud that consisted of creating new transactions and new accounts continuously, to cover up a systematic programme of embezzlements. The operations manager involved created such a complex network of fictitious transactions that he had to forgo holidays to avoid being found out. In the end he made a simple error that led to the discovery of the fraud and the revelation in court that the thief had seen very little of the money himself, as it had been squandered in obscure business ventures by his partners outside the bank.

Probably the best known case is the fraud carried out by a man called Rifkin on the Security Pacific Bank in Los Angeles in 1979. Rifkin, a systems analyst, impersonated a bank officer to use the bank's computer to transfer just over US $10 million to his own account in New York. He used the money to buy US $8 million worth of diamonds in Switzerland and smuggled them back into the US to sell them, a task he found very difficult. By this time the fraud had been discovered and the bank recovered a substantial amount of its losses. While on bail Rifkin attempted to carry out a similar fraud, but was prevented by the FBI.

It is worth reflecting that most of those who have been caught have been discovered by accident or because of their own stupidity. Banks are by no means the only places that suffer from computer crime. The first case of computer crime to come up at the Old Bailey was at the end of 1982 and involved a mother and son who had stolen some £14,000 from the local authority that the mother worked for. It is inconceivable that computers had not been used before that time in the UK for criminal purposes and it is certain that they will be used much more extensively in the future.

Another significant problem is how to stop unauthorised people gaining hold of software and either using it without paying or selling it to third parties. Copyright law concerning software is confused, particularly in the UK where software is still a rather new concept for the legal profession to grasp. British Airways, when it was still BOAC, spent considerable amounts of time and money inventing a computerised reservation system, only to find competitors installing carbon copies as a result of information sold by its employees to a software house. Software is only worth something to the person who cannot copy it easily, thus packaged software is often impossible to copy, and if you bend your disc, you lose the £300 or £400 you paid. However, sooner or later bit copiers (that decode and copy every byte of information) appear that can break any system down and are themselves easily obtainable – a case can be made to justify the existence of bit copiers, as they can be used to recover damaged data discs.

For the treasurer part of the problem of security arises from the relatively casual way that instructions are passed between customer and bank, reflecting the increasing importance of the telephone as a means of communication and the tradition of 'my word is my bond' that is essential for quick response to customers' requirements. While insurance covers many aspects of bank fraud, one area that is still relatively uncertain covers fraud caused by telephone-initiated funds transfer – one good reason for looking for more secure ways of passing those instructions, such as terminal-based communications systems. Banks are covered against fraud committed by their own employees, the cause of the greatest part of bank fraud, but the apparent ease of getting into communications networks exposes the banking system to new problems.

Preventing fraud

Designing systems should always take into account the risk of fraud, malicious damage or breakdown that the system exposes the company to. Automation reduces the interaction between individuals and removes the traditional checks and balances that existed in manual operations. Today's criminal has far more opportunity to work in solitude and stealing from a computer seems to carry far less stigma that other types of crime. A cup of coffee spilt down the back of the machine, either by accident or by design, could stop a business in its tracks. Systems design should anticipate all these possibilities and have the necessary contingencies built-in to cope with them.

The banking system has always worried about fraud and every bank takes great pains to disassociate itself as much as possible from the actions of people outside the bank itself. Opening a current account for a company requires a mandate from the company which bears the signature of those authorised to operate the account, a copy of a board resolution approving the mandate and a copy of the company's memorandum and articles of association, to ensure that the company has the legal right to open the account. These restrictions are not intended to protect the bank, which may be lending funds to the account holder, but the company itself, as it would be liable for any unauthorised withdrawal from the account.

Signature verification has always been the main system of defence, but this is of little use for corporations who normally want to be able to move money quickly by making a telephone call to the bank. Where there is an arrangement for a company to move funds by telephone transfer, the bank will look to limit its liability if an unauthorised person in the company gives telephoned instructions. This sort of problem increases with electronic terminals that can be used to originate transfers.

The main form of security is the use of passwords that can be recognised by the main computer, which will be able to prevent the operator from giving unauthorised instructions. Each holder of a password can have different powers and it is possible to have more than one electronic signature to authorise payments. Passwords can be private to the individuals that use them and should be changed frequently, as people can get careless in keeping them to themselves. Management of passwords is definitely the responsibility of the user rather than the bank.

The new electronic banking terminals can only be used by the bank and its customers: using them to send information to third parties usually infringes the monopoly of the local PTT. Other considerations that should be clearly defined are who provides and maintains the equipment needed and what happens if the equipment malfunctions or breaks down. Again, what happens if the communications equipment breaks down and messages are not properly transmitted should also be defined. These commercial problems are exacerbated by the general lack of clearly agreed legal precedents or rulings.

These problems do not just concern companies, but also involve individual users of financial services from banks and savings companies. As we have seen, more and more banking services are being delivered over automated tellers and in the near future home banking terminals, using home computers and the telephone service, will become commonplace. Security in giving instructions is only one problem. The other main problem will be preventing unauthorised people from getting information, for example, confidential details of personal bank accounts.

CHAPTER 17

The future

We have been looking at the development of two quite different, but closely connected, businesses: one centered on technology and the other on money. Both are difficult enough to understand at the best of times and both have taken a trend towards rapid change and fragmentation. Changes in treasury management centre on the reduction of uncertainty, particularly that caused by volatility of rates and prices in the financial markets.

With technology, the convergence of computer science with telecommunications means that early obsolescence of newly bought equipment is a real problem. No less a problem are the promises made by suppliers for new developments that are at an advanced stage, but have yet to go into production. Delivery could be delayed due to unforeseen problems and these delays could seriously affect completion of projects. To be safe many managers will buy from IBM; no large company is likely to fire a manager for buying the wrong or suddenly out-of-date IBM computer – or most other forms of office equipment made by that company. The more adventurous will look to improve performance or reduce cost by buying from someone smaller who hopefully will be trying harder.

We will see the struggle for the electronic office fought out between two industries, the computer industry and the communications companies. Digital communications bring the PTTs and the virtual monopolies that even a denationalised British Telecom will represent into direct conflct with the computer companies. They, in turn, have simultaneously realised the central role that communications play in the whole business of information technology. The wired society and the electronic village are the sorts of phrases used by the visionaries to describe the future. Much of the technology is around already and further trends may be discerned. For example:

1. Wristwatch-sized television sets are on sale, albeit with rather large power packs.
2. Microcomputers that fit in a briefcase, weigh only a few pounds, work on long-life batteries and come equipped with basic software are available from several manufacturers.
3. Cordless telephones with full ranges of aids, such as preselected dialling, are available for home use. Some of this equipment is very sophisticated.
4. The development of cellular radio which makes much better use of the

airwaves has come at a time when it was widely expected that radio could not expand further as a communications medium due to overcrowding of existing space for channels.

5. Laser discs that can hold incredible amounts of data are the most promising of several methods of replacing existing data storage on hard discs or tapes.

6. Home television sets are now available which produce hard copy of a picture on the screen through a printer built into the console of the set itself.

The technology of the amusement arcade may lead the way into the future, as it did in the development of home computers. A slump in demand for video games in the US has seen major improvements announced for the hardware. Games will be played against a background provided from a laser-read video disc which has the advantage of being able to move from one frame to another on a different part of the disc quickly and smoothly. Thus, you can fly your aeroplane against a background of scenes actually filmed from a similar aircraft, make a decision and the program branches to scenes from a different part of the disc. Interactive voice systems are under trial allowing the player to give verbal instructions to the machine, leaving both hands free to operate the controls. The types of memory storage and voice-activated devices will be an integral part of future office systems.

Changes in the office

The pace of change will not slow down. In the office it will mean the eventual standardisation of equipment specifications, not unlike the use of standard-sized paper and envelopes, which will permit the introduction of inter-office and intercompany electronic mail. The relationship between individual jobs will change. A modern secretary is far more comfortable with the technology than a company boss, having had first-hand experience of computers and the other machines that have been springing up. The role of the secretary as the one who writes may be redefined if the boss takes to typing his own memoranda while the secretary is occupied with managing the flow of information rather than with creating it directly.

Changes in the financial markets

And what of money? Information means power and prior information means wealth. The Rothschilds made one of their fortunes by hearing first about the outcome of the battle of Waterloo and the fact that they were the first to hear was no accident. As the markets have grown so have communications. Perhaps that growth must be limited by the ability of the communications network to grow at the same speed or faster. Certainly the most impressive developments in communications, outside national defence, are in the financial markets, where companies have invested enormous sums in moving information around the world.

A pound is still a pound, although its physical appearance changes, usually for the worse, every few years. The way a pound is used, however, has changed far more rapidly than the way it looks. Some of this change has come from a change in governmental attitudes. The lifting of exchange controls in 1979 meant that a pound need no longer be a pound, but could now easily be a dollar or a franc. Fundamental changes in the way national economies were managed – monetarism in the US and the UK, socialism in France – together with increasing political uncertainty – generated violent swings in interest and exchange rates, forcing up levels of activity in the already busy financial markets around the world.

A whole new range of products is emerging to help treasurers to manage uncertainty. These include financial futures, options and swaps. Financial futures exchanges form a parallel to the money and foreign exchange markets and treat money products as commodities. With options, they provide insurance through alternative ways of hedging interest rate or exchange rate exposure. Swaps are used to convert fixed-rate debt into floating rate debt, or vice versa, or to fix long-dated foreign exchange rates outside the foreign exchange markets, with the principals dealing through a banking intermediary. All these new products offer opportunities for the user, but need to be evaluated both mathematically and commercially. This evaluation can be long and complex, but is usually worth while.

To evaluate these new products and so cope with the demands of the markets as they develop, financial managers have come to rely increasingly on the use of computers to reduce costs and increase productivity. Many cost savings from technology are yet to come, as are the benefits of improved services.

Effects on privacy

We may or may not feel comfortable about the way these improvements can affect our lives. For example, American Express now has a global communications capability that enables it to approve from a single computer in Arizona over 250,000 credit card transactions a day from all over the world; these approvals are made in around five seconds. By centralising its communications activities it can improve efficiencies and enhance its range of services. At the same time, it can get to know a lot more about its individual customers, particularly if it also sells them travellers cheques and insurance. If you want to follow someone's progress around a country what better way than to monitor his use of his credit card? It tells you where he has been, what he has bought and where he is going. There is an old story that tells of a sudden interest in credit cards among the stalwarts of the Communist Party in Russia, not because they wanted people to spend more, but because of the control over people's actions that the use of credit cards could bring. Perhaps we should take comfort in the stubborn refusal of the UK workman to take anything but cash in return for his labours.

Invasion of privacy presupposes that you have a privacy that other people want to invade. In Western society that tends to happen when a rule, particularly the law, has been broken and it could be argued that those most vociferous in seeking privacy may be those who have something to hide. Each of us has a file somewhere, in the tax office, the doctor's surgery or the police station. It will only be a matter of time before all these data bases will be linked together and only the inefficiencies of the people filing the information will protect individuals from the eyes of the marketing men and the political activists, the former to bombard selected targets with promotional material, the latter to drum up votes from those with a socio-economic profile that fits the party in question.

Artificial intelligence

The most radical change that can be foreseen is the distribution of very cheap, but powerful, computer capability. This will take software into realms of sophistication far beyond our present experience. Again the trends are firmly established. In medical matters it appears that people will happily tell a computer things they may not tell a doctor to his face, in much the same way that people can be observed queuing up for a cash dispenser in a banking hall when the tellers' windows are unoccupied, because they feel more at ease with the machine. The computer itself can exhaustively question the patient and can use data from tests performed on the patient to arrive at a diagnosis that is better than that of even a quite experienced physician. This is because the computer can be fed with massive amounts of data and can be taught to correlate new data against existing knowledge.

Teaching computers to think for themselves became necessary when it became evident that computers were having a very hard time beating mere mortals at chess. The conclusion was that as humans do not think rationally all the time, they can make leaps of logic without having painstakingly to examine every possible alternative. The brain sees situations in the context of similar situations from the past. Some experiences are possibly so deeply rooted as to appear to be tribal memories. Thus, the brain can instantly recall how it dealt with this situation in the previous encounters with similar problems and can postulate how to better that performance this time around. Learning from experience is the only way that thought processes can be short cut – unfortunately, this requires considerable processing capacity if computers are involved.

The present interest of technicians in super-computers is to bring such processing capacity to bear on a problem, so that something approaching the flexibility of the human mind can be combined with the mindless efficiency of a computer. Once we can find a way to solve the problem on a big machine then we can try to solve it on a smaller scale. Essentially we will be able to let the machine make decisions for us on total or partial evidence. Working backwards from the answer is something that computers are not very good at unless they are very carefully programmed.

The implication for the individual of all this artificial intelligence is that he can use a machine to control his activities. For example, his home computer will keep his budget and this will be programmed with certain parameters as to the maximum amount of credit that is available to the individual. The home computer will talk regularly with other computers and data bases, such as those in a bank or a government agency. The home computer will contain a level of artificial intelligence that will enable it to do certain things that we may now find odd. If it has worked out the budget, it may find that only a certain amount can be spent on electricity. It will therefore keep heating to a level that it estimates it can afford, having consulted with the computer in the weather bureau as to the likely temperature over the budget period and compared this with the heating levels normally maintained in the house. These will be compared with the norm for the region, obtained from the computers of the gas and electricity boards, and the computer will suggest a level of warmth that is lower, but hopefully still comfortable, and will be within the projected cost constraint for this one utility.

When the house-owner goes into a shop and makes a purchase way in excess of his budgeted spending, he will pay for his purchase with a credit card. This will be fed into an electronic reader on the side of the cash till. The till will automatically call the bank which, in turn, will call the home computer. The home computer may 'feel' strongly enough to refuse payment until the purchaser has countered the computer's objection by keying in an overriding password through the cash till. If prompted, the computer could advise why it did not like the transaction and could explain the basis used to draw up the budget. Its arguments will be based on the level of savings, future income and projected costs, probably derived from average cost levels relating to other individuals in the same income bracket.

The computer will learn as it goes along. Each new change in legislation will be picked up from the government data base. Picking the most efficient tax structure will be a major preoccupation. The home budgeting process will be but one of a wide range of services provided by the computer, including shopping, and possibly working, from home.

In the financial markets, computers will be used to speed up reactions and to work quietly away on problems, such as when would be the best time to execute a particular trade. Again they will be able to structure basic rules based on past experience and suggest ways to improve the approach to trading currently adopted by the treasurer or the dealer. The ability to pool information will certainly see an increase in the netting of intercompany cash flows that will both reduce the pressure on the banking system and increase the efficiency of the overall markets. It will be very interesting to see what will happen as these developments unfold.

Conclusion

Most managers need to find out more about the technology that is invading their everyday work. A book can whet your appetite, but the best way is to read the manuals of the computers that are being used in the office or to buy computers for yourself, either in the home or in the office. It is difficult to recommend any literature on the subject, as the equipment available is so varied and each user will have a different need and a different inclination as to how far he will want to be involved with the detail of the machine, such as the writing of programs. To repeat what was said in the Introduction, there is no substitute for hands-on experience and that experience is essential if we are to profit from the changes that are taking place around us.

The treasurer in particular has the opportunity to benefit from technological developments. Cash is the lifeblood of the company and its management requires the best available computer and communications facilities. These facilities will improve and change dramatically over the next few years. Installation of systems is just as critical a management task as management of exposures and positions in the market. A key factor will be the ability to communicate systems specifications clearly and to educate the technologists in the specialised requirements of the financial markets. Money lends itself to computerisation. Most of the cash in the world takes the form of electronic blips, either in a computer or moving along the wires between one computer and another. As money and technology become increasingly interlinked, the management of one requires an understanding of the other.

APPENDIX

Bankers' acceptances arbitrage by Graham Simister and Michael Smith — November 1983

```
100 '
120 '
140 '
160 '
180 '
200 '    CALLING PROGRAM IN LINES 100 - 700
220 '    ROUTINES IN 1000 - 51000
240 '
260 '    Input start up data
280 KEY OFF:WIDTH 80
300 CLS:LOCATE 12,29:PRINT"*** Check PRINTER ***"
320 FOR T = 1 TO 2500:NEXT
340 CLS:LOCATE 5,5:PRINT"NOTE:    RAC= Reserve asset cost which is automatically
                          added to sterling libo"
360 LOCATE 8,5:PRINT"    TODAY'S DATE is system date for PC-DOS"
361 LOCATE 9,5:PRINT "    SPOT is current $/ exchange rate"
362 LOCATE 10,5:PRINT "    Under SWAP enter left and right hand side rates"
363 LOCATE 11,5:PRINT "    ???? indicates data entry should be rekeyed"
380 LOCATE 12,5:PRINT"    PRESS (ESC) to correct entries:move cursor under
                          entry to be corrected"
400 LOCATE 20,5:PRINT"PRESS ANY KEY TO CONTINUE"
420 A$=INKEY$: IF A$="" THEN 420
440 GOSUB 2700
460 GOSUB 2940
480 TODAY$ = MID$(DATE$,N4,N2)+LEFT$(DATE$,N2)+RIGHT$(DATE$,N2):LOCATE 2,37:PRIN
T FN FORMAT$(TODAY$):
500 '
520 LOCATE 3,3:PRINT "Enter Rac cost: "::CV=3:CH19:CC=196:A1=N4:GOSUB 2220:IF A
$=ES$ THEN 520 ELSE IF AN$ = " " AND RAC THEN 540 ELSE IF AN$="" THEN 520 ELSE RA
C=VAL(AN$)
540 LOCATE 3,3:PRINT "        (Rac:";RAC;BS$;")";
560 LOCATE 24,3:PRINT SPC(N20)::CV=3:CH=54:CC=46:GOSUB 2420:IF A$=ES$ THEN 520 E
LSE IF AN$="" AND VALUES$"" THEN 620 ELSE AN$=AN$+MID$(TODAY$,LEN(AN$)+N1):GOSUB
 2620:IF NOT ER THEN LOCATE CV,CH:PRINT"What ???"::FOR X = 1 TO 1000:NEXT:GOTO 5
60
580 LASTDATE$=AN$:ARG1!=FNDN!(YEAR+1900,MONTH,NDAYS)
600 VALUE$=AN$:LOCATE 2,54:PRINT FN FORMAT$(VALUES$);
620 CV=3:CH=70:CC=196:A1=N8:GOSUB 2220:IF A$=ES$ THEN 560 ELSE IF AN$ = " " AND S
POT THEN 680 ELSE IF AN$="" THEN 620 ELSE LOCATE 2,70:PRINT AN$:SPC(A1-LEN(AN$))
::SPOT=VAL(AN$)
640 '
660 '
680 '    Input period data
700 '
720 PRD=N1
740 CV=N5+PRD*N2
760 IF PRD=N5 THEN 1260 ELSE IF PRD)N1 THEN BEEP:LOCATE 2,3:PRINT"Press (C) to c
alc:"::GOSUB 2600:IF A$="C" OR A$="c" THEN 1260 ELSE IF A$=ES$ THEN PRD=PRD-N1:C,
V=CV-N2:GOTO 1180
780 ' Enter date and calc date diffs
800 CH=3:CC=46:GOSUB 2420:IF A$=ES$ AND PRD=N1 THEN 620 ELSE IF A$=ES$ THEN 760
820 IF AN$="" AND DAYS(PRD) THEN 880
840 AN$=AN$+MID$(LASTDATE$,LEN(AN$)+N1):GOSUB 2640:IF NOT ER THEN LOCATE CV,CH:P
RINT"What ???"::FOR X=1 TO 500:NEXT:GOTO 800
860 LASTDATE$=AN$:ARG2!=FNDN!(YEAR+1900,MONTH,NDAYS):DAYS(PRD)=ARG2!-ARG1!::IF DA
YS(PRD)(N1 THEN BEEP:GOTO 800 ELSE LOCATE CV-N1,CH:PRINT LEFT$(AN$,N2)+"/"+MID$C
AN$,N3,N2)::LOCATE CV-N1,9:PRINT DAYS(PRD);
880 ' enter swap rates
```

```
900 CH=14:CC=196:A1=N4:GOSUB 2220:IF A$=ES$ THEN 800 ELSE IF AN$="" AND LSWAP(PR
D) THEN 940 ELSE IF AN$="" THEN 900
920 LSWAP(PRD)=VAL(AN$):LOCATE CV-N1,CH:PRINT SPC(N5)::LOCATE CV-N1,CH:PRINT LSW
AP(PRD)
940 CH=19:A1=N4:GOSUB 2220:IF A$=ES$ THEN 900 ELSE IF AN$="" AND RSWAP(PRD) THEN
 1000 ELSE IF AN$="" THEN 940
960 RSWAP(PRD)=VAL(AN$):LOCATE CV-N1,CH:PRINT SPC(N5)::LOCATE CV-N1,CH:PRINT RSW
AP(PRD)::IF RSWAP(PRD)<LSWAP(PRD) THEN RSWAP(PRD)=-RSWAP(PRD):LSWAP(PRD)=-LSWAP(
PRD)
980 '   enter $ba
1000 CH=25:A1=N5:GOSUB 2220:IF A$=ES$ THEN 940 ELSE IF AN$="" AND DBA(PRD) THEN
1060 ELSE IF AN$="" THEN 1000
1020 DBA(PRD)=VAL(AN$):LOCATE CV-N1,CH:PRINT SPC(N6)::LOCATE CV-N1,CH:PRINT USIN
G PV$;DBA(PRD):
1040 '  enter st ba
1060 CH=32:GOSUB 2220:IF A$=ES$ THEN 1000 ELSE IF AN$="" AND SBA(PRD) THEN 1120
ELSE IF AN$="" THEN 1060
1080 SBA(PRD)=VAL(AN$):LOCATE CV-N1,CH:PRINT SPC(N6)::LOCATE CV-N1,CH:PRINT USIN
G PV$;SBA(PRD):
1100 '  enter $li
1120 CH=39:GOSUB 2220:IF A$=ES$ THEN 1060 ELSE IF AN$="" AND DLI(PRD) THEN 1180
ELSE IF AN$="" THEN 1120
1140 DLI(PRD)=VAL(AN$):LOCATE CV-N1,CH:PRINT SPC(N6)::LOCATE CV-N1,CH:PRINT USIN
G PV$;DLI(PRD):
1160 '  enter st li
1180 CH=46:CC=196:GOSUB 2220:IF A$=ES$ THEN 1120 ELSE IF AN$="" AND SLI(PRD) THE
N 1220 ELSE IF AN$="" THEN 1180
1200 SLI(PRD)=VAL(AN$)+RAC:LOCATE CV-N1,CH:PRINT SPC(N6)::LOCATE CV-N1,CH:PRINT
USING PV$;SLI(PRD):
1220 PRD=PRD+N1:GOTO 740
1240 '
1260 ' Calculate results
1280 '  get yields
1300 FOR X=N1 TO PRD-N1
1320 DBY(X) = DBA(X)/(N1 - DBA(X) * DAYS(X)/BASEUS)
1340 SBY(X) = SBA(X)/(N1 - SBA(X) * DAYS(X)/BASEUK)
1360 NEXT
1380 '  get swapped cost
1400 FOR X=N1 TO PRD-N1
1420 DSB(X)=((SBY(X)*DAYS(X)/BASEUK)+N1)*(SPOT+RSWAP(X)/TENM):DSB(X)=(DSB(X)-SPO
T)*BASEUS/(DAYS(X)*SPOT)
1440 SDB(X)=((SPOT*DAYS(X)*DBY(X)/BASEUS)+SPOT)/(SPOT+LSWAP(X)/TENM):SDB(X)=(SDB
(X)-N1)*(BASEUK/DAYS(X))
1460 NEXT
1480 '  get diffs
1500 FOR X=N1 TO PRD-N1
1520 RE1(X)=DLI(X)-DBY(X)
1540 RE2(X)=SLI(X)-SBY(X)
1560 RE3(X)=SLI(X)-SDB(X)
1580 RE4(X)=SBY(X)-SDB(X)
1600 RE5(X)=DLI(X)-DSB(X)
1620 NEXT
1640 '   Display on screen
1660 '
1680 '   display yields and swap results
1700 FOR X=N1 TO PRD-N1
720 CV=N4+X*N2
1740 LOCATE CV,53:PRINT USING PU$;DBY(X):LOCATE CV,59:PRINT USING PU$;SBY(X):LOC
ATE CV,65:PRINT USING PU$;SDB(X):LOCATE CV,72:PRINT USING PU$;DSB(X)
1760 NEXT
1780 '   now display diffs
1800 FOR X=N1 TO PRD-N1
1820 CV=N14+X*N2
1840 LOCATE CV,4:PRINT DAYS(X):LOCATE CV,15:PRINT USING PU$;RE1(X):LOCATE CV,28:
PRINT USING PU$;RE2(X):LOCATE CV,40:PRINT USING PU$;RE3(X):LOCATE CV,52:PRINT US
ING PU$;RE4(X):LOCATE CV,64:PRINT USING PU$;RE5(X)
1860 NEXT
1880 LOCATE 2,3:PRINT SPC(N19)::LOCATE 24,3:PRINT "Waiting for (SHIFT-PrtSc) or
(P) "::GOSUB 2600:IF A$="P" OR A$="p" THEN 1920
1900 GOTO 680
1920 ' Print instructions
1940 CLS
1960 LOCATE 2,5:PRINT"*** KEY ***"
1980 LOCATE 4,5:PRINT"Dba/Dlibo ... dollar libo minus dollar ba yield"
2000 LOCATE 6,5:PRINT"Sba/Slibo ... stg libo minus stg ba yield"
2020 LOCATE 8,5:PRINT"Sfs/Slibo ... stg libo minus fully swapped stg from dollar
 ba"
2040 LOCATE 10,5:PRINT"Sfs/Sba   ... stg ba minus fully swapped stg from dollar
ba"
2060 LOCATE 12,5:PRINT"Dfs/Dlibo ... dollar libo minus fully swapped dollars fro
m sterling ba"
```

```
2080 LOCATE 14,5:PRINT"Dbay and Sbay are dollar and sterling ba yields"
2100 LOCATE 16,5:PRINT"D/sba and S/dba are dollar and sterling costs,"
2120 LOCATE 17,5:PRINT"fully swapped from sterling and dollar ba's"
2140 LOCATE 20,5:PRINT"-------------------------------------------------------
-------"
2160 LOCATE 24,3:PRINT "Waiting for (SHIFT-PrtSc) ";:GOSUB 2600
2180 RUN "MENU"
2200 LOCATE 21,5:PRINT"-------------------------------------------------------
-------------"
2220 '  Alpha - Numeric Input Routine
2240 A=NO:AN$="":LOCATE CV,CH:PRINT STRING$(A1,CC);
2260 '
2280 LOCATE CV,CH+A,N1:A$=INKEY$:IF A$="" THEN 2280 ELSE IF INSTR(LEGAL1$,A$) TH
EN 2300 ELSE ON INSTR(LEGAL2$,A$) GOTO 2940,2380,2380,2320,2360,2360:GOTO 2260
2300 IF A=A1 THEN 2260 ELSE AN$=AN$+A$:A=A+N1:PRINT A$;:GOTO 2280
2320 IF A=NO THEN 2260 ELSE IF A=N1 THEN AN$="" ELSE AN$=MID$(AN$,N1,A-N1)
2340 A=A-N1:LOCATE CV,CH+A:PRINT CHR$(CC);:GOTO 2280
2360 IF A$="." AND INSTR(AN$,".") THEN 2260 ELSE IF A$="-" AND INSTR(AN$,"-") TH
EN 2260 ELSE IF A$="-" AND A ) NO THEN 2260 ELSE 2300
2380 LOCATE CV,CH:PRINT SPC(A1);:RETURN       leave routine with result in AN$
2400 '
2420 '   Formatted input routine
2440 AN$="":NO:LOCATE CV,CH,N1:PRINT AF$;
2460 IF A=LEN(AF$) THEN 2520 ELSE A=INSTR(A+N1,AF$,CHR$(CC)):LOCATE CV,CH+A-N1:P
RINT"";
2480 A$=INKEY$:IF A$="" THEN 2480 ELSE IF INSTR(LEGAL1$,A$) THEN PRINT A$;:AN$ =
AN$+A$:GOTO 2460
2500 ON INSTR(LEGAL2$,A$) GOTO 2940,2560,2560,2440
2520 '
2540 A$=INKEY$:IF A$="" THEN 2540 ELSE IF A+LEN(AF$) THEN 2500 ELSE 2480
2560 LOCATE CV,CH:PRINT SPC(LEN(AF$)):RETURN   An$ contains result
2580 '  Wait for kybd input
2600 A$=INKEY$:IF A$="" THEN 2600 ELSE RETURN
620 '  Check date entry
2640 NDAYS=VAL(LEFT$(AN$,N2)):MONTH=VAL(MID$(AN$,N3,N2)):YEAR=VAL(RIGHT$(AN$,N2)
)
2660 ER = (NDAYS)NO AND NDAYS(N32) AND MONTH)NO AND MONTH(N13) AND (YEAR)=VAL (R
IGHT$(TODAY$,N2)))
2680 RETURN
2700 '   Initialise variables
2720 '
2740 DEFINT N,M,Y,A,X
2760 NO=0:N1=1:N2=2:N3=3:N4=4:N5=5:N6=6:N7=7:N8=8:N9=9:N10=10:N11=11:N12=12:N13=
13:N14=14:N15=15:N16=16:N17=17:N18=18:N19=19:N20=20:N21=21:N22=22:N23=23:N24=24:
N25=25:N26=26:N27=27:N28=28:N29=29:N30=30:N31=31:N32=32
2780 AF$="../../.." :LEGAL1$="0123456789":LEGAL2$="\"+CHR$(13)+CHR$(27)+CHR$(8)+"
"+"-":ES$=CHR$(27):BS$=CHR$(29):PU$="£££.££":PV$="££.££"
2800 BASEUS=36000!:BASEUK=36500!:TENM=10000
2820 DIM SCR$(23)
2840   Calculate a computational date
2860 DEF FN DN!(YEAR%,MONTH%,NDAYS%) = YEAR% * 365 + INT((YEAR%-1)/4)+(MONTH%-1)
*28+VAL(MID$("000303060811131619212426",(MONTH%-1)*2+1,2))-((MONTH%)2)AND((YEAR%
AND NOT -4)=0)+NDAYS%
2880 '  Print a format date
2900 DEF FN FORMAT$(AN$) = LEFT$(AN$,N2)+"/"+MID$(AN$,N3,N2)+"/"+RIGHT$(AN$,N2)
2920 RETURN
2940 LIN$ = "........................................................................
..........."
2960 TEX$(1)="    Val    Days    Swap      Dba     Sba     Dli     Sli     Dbay   Sbay  S
Dba   D/Sba"
2980 TEX$(2)="                                Today:          Value:              Soo
 :"
3000 TEX$(3)=" Periods      Dba/Dlibo    Sba/Slibo    Sfs/Slibo    Sfs/Sba    Df
s/Dlibo"
3020 CLS:LOCATE 1,1:PRINT LIN$
3060 LOCATE 5,1:PRINT LIN$
3080 LOCATE 2,1:PRINT TEX$(2)
3100 LOCATE 4,1:PRINT TEX$(1)
3120 LOCATE 14,1:PRINT TEX$(3)
3140 LOCATE 15,1:PRINT LIN$
3160 LOCATE 23,1:PRINT LIN$
3180 FOR X = 2 TO 23:LOCATE X,1:PRINT":":NEXT :FOR X = 2 TO 22:LOCATE X,80:PRINT
":":NEXT
3200 FOR X = 6 TO 13:LOCATE X,52:PRINT":":NEXT
3220 LOCATE 1,80:PRINT".":LOCATE 23,80:PRINT":";
3240 RETURN
```

Index